THE COMPLETE
ENCYCLOPEDIA OF
BUTTERFLIES

THE COMPLETE
ENCYCLOPEDIA OF
BUTTERFLIES

Describes the development and life cycle of butterflies
from around the world

WIJBREN LANDMAN

REBO
PUBLISHERS

© 1999 Rebo International b.v., Lisse, The Netherlands

Text: Wijbren Landman
Photographs: Wijbren Landman, Matthijs Kuijpers, Jelle de Vire
Cover design: Minkowsky Graphics, The Netherlands
Editor: Gerda Leegsma, The Netherlands
Production: TextCase, The Netherlands
Typesseting and layout: Hof&Land Typografie, The Netherlands

ISBN 90 366 1587 9

Table of Contents

Argema mittrei

Introduction

What is a butterfly?

Butterflies have a special place in the insect world. The use of names such as flying flowers or flying jewels indicates that butterflies in general are considered as being beautiful, elusive and fascinating. In many cultures the influence of butterflies is not limited to earthly existence.

For the ancient Greeks, for example the word "psyche" meant butterfly as well as soul. They believed that when the soul leaves the body of the deceased, it flies to heaven like a butterfly.

Even now butterflies are usually appreciated very differently to their close relatives, the insects.

In the first place almost everybody finds butterflies beautiful. They have magnificent colours and fly cheerfully from flower to flower in the sun. They do not bite or sting. Nor are they able to, because they do not have the necessary mouth parts. This is certainly not true of most other insects. Think of wasps, beetles, grasshoppers and mosquitoes. In contrast to these creatures, the butterfly is a model of innocence.

Bird Spider

The insects

The insects belong to the largest phylum of the animal kingdom, the Arthropods. The Crustacea (lobsters, crabs and wood lice), the Arachnids (spiders, scorpions, mites and harvestmen) and the Centipede-like insects (millipedes and centipedes) are also classified in this group. The insects are the largest group represented within this diverse group of animals. They form by far the largest and most richly varied group in the animal kingdom. No less than 70% of the over 1 million species described are insects. The main features that all these generally small animals have in common are: 6 legs, 1 pair of antennae and a segmented body of which a head, a thorax and an abdomen can be distinguished. The insects are subdivided in thirty so-called

Anterica rabena, *caterpillar*

Graphium weiskei

Greta Oro, *butterfly*

Ephippiger

orders, mainly on the basis of their wing features. Some of these orders are the Coleoptera (beetles), Hymenoptera (bees, wasps and ants), Orthoptera (grasshoppers and crickets) and the Lepidoptera (butterflies and moths).

Lepidoptera

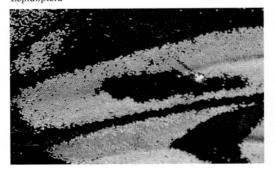

Butterflies and moths

Butterflies and moths are classified under the Lepidoptera. After the beetles,

Long-horned beetle

Siproeta epaphus

Longnicornia Moth

the Lepidoptera form the order with the largest number of species. Up to now, no less than 16,000 species of Lepidoptera have been described. For this encyclopaedia, a presentable choice has made out of this staggering number. To maintain an overview, it is important to have a good system by which to classify all these Lepidoptera. In the biological system, an order is divided into families, a family into genera and a genus into species. The same classification is also used in this encyclopaedia. Lepidoptera have always been distinguished into but-terflies and moths. The distinction is made on basis of the shape of the antennae. The Lepidoptera with threadlike antennae ending in a small knot are butterflies. The Lepidoptera with differently shaped antennae, for example threadlike, pectinate or feathery, are all classified as moths. Most butterflies are brightly coloured and active during the daytime, while moths have dull colours and are active at night. This, however, is a rule with many exceptions.

Automeris aurantiaca *from Argentina*

Caterpillar of the Papilio aegeus

1 Build

The body of a caterpillar, as of all insects, consists of a head, a thorax and an abdomen. A caterpillar is mainly a gorging machine. It is built rather simply. Actually it consists of not much more than a head with 13 segments behind it. The most striking feature of the head is

Emperor Moth from Papua New Guinea

Caterpillar of the Inachis, *the Peacock*

the large jaws. The caterpillar uses these to chew and consume large amounts of food in a short time. Between the jaws are glands that produce a liquid from which silk can be made. On both sides of the jaws are two small antennae with a number of simply constructed eyes,

Close-up of a butterfly head

called ocelli. A few real legs are attached to each of the first three (thorax) segments. They are used more for grasping the food than for transport. The so-called abdominal prolegs legs are attached to segments 6 to 9, while the last segment has the large hind prolegs. With all these legs, which are provided with small hooks, a caterpillar can walk very well and can hold on tightly to a plant. Openings are clearly distinguishable on the sides of each segment. These give access to a system of tubes which are part of the

Saturnia zuleika

caterpillar's breathing mechanism. Caterpillars have a body which is either bald or provided with hairs, spines, tails, etcetera, depending on the species.

The body of a butterfly or moth also has the typical build of an insect with a head, a thorax and abdomen. On the head there are some remarkable organs, of which the antennae, the proboscis and the compound eyes are the most prominent. The antennae on each side of the head, are not just balancing organs and feelers, but are mainly used as a nose for

Pollen on the proboscis of a Heliconias

The beautiful colours of the Siproeta stelenes

the butterfly or moth. With their extremely sensitive antennae, Emperor Moth males can smell a female of their species from a distance of many miles. They have the most sensitive noses of the whole animal kingdom.

Butterflies and moths are also equipped with a proboscis. This is, as it were, a straw with which they sucks up their food, and which is rolled up when not in use. Because butterflies and moths do not have jaws to bite or chew with, they have to rely on liquid food. They suck it up with their proboscis. The most important liquid food is nectar from flowers, but some butterflies and moths also like the juice of rotting fruit, dead animals, manure or urine.

Heliconias sometimes collect pollen which sticks to their proboscis. They make the proteins of that pollen soluble and then suck them up through their proboscis. In that way they are able to use solid food as a source of nutrition. Such a way of absorbing food is exceptional among butterflies. Some Lepi-

Morpho adonis

doptera have a short proboscis, not even a centimetre long, while for other Lepidoptera, such as the Convolvulus Hawk-Moth, 15 centimetres is no exception. The Emperor Moth family and some other families of moths have to make do without a proboscis. These moths do not visit flowers, so they do not absorb food and therefore do not live very long, usually not longer than a few days.

Morpho portis *with one blue-highlighted wing*

The eyes of a butterfly or moth are composed of a large number of small eyes, the ocelli. Eyes having such a structure can detect movements particularly well, for example of a bird rapidly closing in, or other danger. And, of course, those of a congener flying about, which might be a suitable candidate for mating. Butterflies can also see colours very well. They find flowers thanks to their colours.

The thorax

The thorax of a butterfly or moth consists of three segments. A few legs are connected to each segment, while a pair of wings is connected to the middle and last segments. Compared to other insects, butterflies and moths have exceptionally large wings. Some species have a wingspan of 30 centimetres, for example the Giant Atlas Moth.

The wings of butterflies and moths are covered with small scales from which the insects derive their name Lepidoptera. The scales, which are arranged on the wings like roof tiles, are hollow and contain pigments. These give the butterfly its beautiful colours. The colour of Purple Emperors does not only depend on the kind of pigment, but also on the structure and the arrangement of the scales. A special form of light refraction is created, giving the wings a metallic glow. Perfect examples of this are the South American Morphos, the male of which has wings with a vivid blue sheen.

Butterflies belonging the family of the Blues even owe their name to the striking blue colour on the wings. Many species of Ornithoptera sometimes have a golden glow on their wings. Because these colours are created by a refraction of light, they do not become pale, not even when the butterfly is dead. This is, however, the case with pigment colours, which turn pale when exposed to light for a long time. You can see this, for example, in butterflies from an old collection in a natural history museum. The colours on the wings can differ widely within a species. Sometimes these are geographical forms, which means that all the individuals in a certain area have the same colour pattern, and each area has butterflies with their own characteristic colour pattern. Many butterflies also have special colour varieties. These can be mutants which lack a certain pigment, such as Coppers with white wings instead of orange ones. A very special anomaly is the so-called lateral gynandromorph. This name means that the butterfly is half male, half female, but in such a way that the dividing line is exactly in the middle. The left half of the

Papilio dardanus, *half male, half female*

insect is of one gender and the right half of the other. A similar situation cannot occur in mammals because their sex is determined differently from that of insects. The basis of the development of a gynandromorph is, as in all other butterflies and moths, a fertilised egg. This can be a cell with two nuclei, a male and a female, or a cell with one nucleus in which an error has occurred during one of the first cell divisions. When such a cell develops into a butterfly, the result of the genetic anomaly is a gynandromorph. Such butterflies remain hidden from the human eye when the colour patterns on the wings are the same for males and females. But in those butterflies for which each sex has its own colour pattern, a gynandromorph can be distinguished immediately. Among the butterflies which are bred in the Tropical Butterfly Garden of the Noorder Dierenpark, this phenomenon is determined with a frequency of 1 in 90,000.

The abdomen

The abdomen is composed of 10 segments, the last 2 or 3 of which are fused together as a genital organ. Males have a pair of pincer-shaped projections at the rear end with which they grasp the female while mating. Female butterflies have an ovipositor, with which they lay eggs on plants. In the female's abdomen there are glands that produce special sex pheromones. These are used to attract males.

Lexias dirtea, *a lateral gynandromorph*

2 The life cycle

Butterflies and moths belong to the winged insects.

These in turn can be divided in two large groups. First of all, the insects with an incomplete metamorphosis. The larvae of these insects which have just crawled out of the egg already look like mature insects. They are just a lot smaller and do not have wings yet in the larval stage. The larva grows with each sloughing and at the last sloughing it gets wings. Then it is fully grown. There is no distinct pupa stage. Grasshoppers, walking sticks and dragonflies have a similar life cycle.

The second group is that of the insects with a complete metamorphosis. The larvae of these insects crawl out of the egg. These larvae do not resemble the mature stage of the insect at all. Think of the maggot, which develops into a fly and, of course, the caterpillar, which eventually becomes a butterfly or moth. Such a larva sloughs several times and becomes a bigger larva each time. At the last sloughing it changes into a pupa. This is the stage in which the insect goes through the so-called metamorphosis, the metamorphosis from a larva into a mature, winged insect. Beetles, wasps, flies as well as butterflies and moths belong to this group of insects. In brief, the life of a butterfly or moth is as follows:

Butterfly/moth → egg →
caterpillar → pupa →
butterfly/moth → egg, etc.

A katydid does not have a pupa stage

Heliconius melpomene, *caterpillar*

Heliconius melpomene, *butterfly visible in the pupae*

Heliconius melpomene, *butterfly just out of the pupae*

Heliconius melpomene, *butterfly with drying wings*

Heliconius melpomene, *butterfly*

Love among the Lepidoptera

Kallima inachus, *old butterfly*

The lives of Lepidoptera are very short. Most of them do not live longer than two or three weeks. In this short time they have to produce offspring. The first step is, of course, to find a congener of the opposite sex to mate with. This is not very easy for butterflies and moths. Worldwide there are more than 160,000 different species, which are often very similar. Nevertheless, butterflies and moths have their methods of getting the right male together with the right female. Female moths sit in between the plants or in another strategic spot and release an aromatic substance with which they lure males from far and near. These lures are called sex pheromones. The speciality of these pheromones is that they are distinctive for a certain butterfly species. Each butterfly species has its own characteristic odour. In some species the males can smell such a pheromone from a large distance. Male Emperor Moths can even smell a female congener from a distance of four kilometres. Butterflies recognise each other first of all by their external appearance. They mainly look for each other in conspicuous places in their habitat, such as a hilltop, a single tree or an open space in the woods. Males fly about madly and throw themselves at every female butterfly that slightly resembles a female of their own species. In doing so, they pay attention to characteristics such as colour, form and size.

When the suitable candidates for mating have approached each other, they begin the courtship. Some butterflies, such as Hairstreaks, do this while flying. Males fly under the females and throw themselves backwards, during which they brush their wings against the antennae of the female. In other species, the female sits on a plant and the male dances directly above her. While dancing he waves a quantity of sex pheromones at his chosen partner. Females are only stimulated to mate by the scents of males of her own species. They simply cannot smell the males of other species. If such a male should try to seduce the female anyway, she would let him know that she is not interested by taking on a char-

Papilio demoleus, *mating*

Actias selene

Cethosia chrysippe

Mating of Heliconius melpomene *with* Heliconius cydno

Eggs of the Caligo memnon

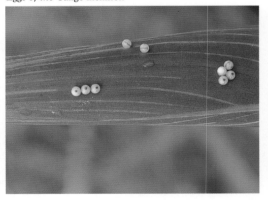

acteristically defensive attitude with her abdomen.

If males and females have made it clear by scents and colours that they belong to the same species, mating usually occurs. It starts with a coupling of the external sex organs. A mating can easily take many hours and for moths it can even go on for a whole twenty-four hours. During copulation, the male does not only pass on sperm cells to the female, but also certain proteins. She uses them for the production of her eggs. The male usually gives off an aromatic substance as well. This makes the female less attractive to any following males, because they prefer odourless and there-fore virgin females.

The egg

After mating the males go looking for other females while the females look for plants on which to lay their eggs. Especially butterflies have a strong preference for plants belonging to a certain species. These so-called host-plants are recognised by a butterfly female with the aid of the sensilla on her legs. Thus, solely by standing on a plant, a female can judge whether the plant is suitable as food for her offspring and therefore for laying her eggs. The size of Lepidoptera eggs varies from a few tenths of a millimetre to almost half a centimetre. Some females lay their eggs one by one on different plants, others lay them in groups. Lepi-

Caterpillars of the Caligo memnon *eat the eggshell first*

The caterpillar of the Ornithoptera priamus

The caterpillar of the Orgyia antiqua

doptera eggs have a hard shell, which can be smooth or have ridges and holes. The shape of the egg is very diverse, and differs from species to species: balls, cones, cylinders, discs, domes, etc.

The embryo develops inside the egg. This process usually takes a few days, sometimes weeks. Eggs often change colour when it is time for the caterpillar to be born.

The caterpillar, a gorging machine

Caterpillars crawl out of Lepidoptera eggs and form a vital link in the life cycle these insects. This is the stage at which growth takes place. Caterpillars are totally built to absorb a large amount of food in a short time. This starts right after birth, when they eat the shell which they have just crawled out of. When they are finished with that, they continue to eat the plant they are on.

Despite their huge appetite, caterpillars are extremely picky. If they cannot eat from the proper host-plant, they will starve before accepting another plant. Fortunately, the female usually lays her eggs on the right host-plant, so the caterpillar can start its meal right after its birth. It eats large amounts of leaves and other foods rapidly. To be able to grow, the caterpillar sheds its skin, or sloughs, a number of times. Its skin is not elastic. If it fills its stomach at a certain stage, it will need a new and wider jacket. It has to slough. To do this, the caterpillar seeks a sheltered spot and spins silk thread with which it fastens its abdomen to a plant. Then its skin tears open at the front and the caterpillar walks out of its old skin. A new skin, which is a few sizes bigger, has already been formed. When the new skin is dry, the caterpillar can continue its meal. In a period of two to three weeks a caterpillar can reach a weight that is a few thousand times its birth weight. Not all caterpillars grow this fast. A Goat Moth caterpillar, for instance, can take over three years to develop. That kind of caterpillar chews passageways in trees and eats wood. The chewing and digesting of such food naturally requires more time than when a caterpillar eats leaves of herbaceous plants. Most caterpillars slough four or five times. At the last sloughing a caterpillar does not appear, but a pupa. For that purpose the caterpillar first spins silk thread onto the plant. There it hooks its back legs into this spun thread and hangs. Some caterpillars, like those of the Hairstreaks, spin a sort of belt around their middle to fasten themselves to the plant. When they have peeled off their skin, they are pupae.

Pupating caterpillar of the Ornithoptera priamus

Papilio caterpillar in the final growth stage

The cocoon of the Attacus atlas

Pupating caterpillar pupae of the Papilio polytes

The pupa and the cocoon

Metamorphosis takes place in the pupa. After a lifetime of eating, the caterpillar changes into a butterfly or moth which is totally focused on reproduction.

The pupa is an extremely vulnerable stage in the life of a butterfly or moth. In an emergency it does not have legs or wings to bring itself to safety. A safe place to pupate is therefore of extreme importance. Pupae of butterflies, which are fastened to plants, are beautifully camouflaged by form and colour. Various caterpillars, like those of the Emperor Moth family, spin a cocoon. This is a covering of a kilometres long silk thread which is wrapped around the caterpillar numerous times, with the threads glued together each time by a kind of adhesive. Inside this safe cocoon, the caterpillar pupates and changes shape. The pupa stage sometimes lasts about ten days, but it can also last three years. This depends on the species of butterfly or moth and on external circumstances such as temperature and humidity.

Just hatched Morpho peleides

Morpho peleides *pumping up its wings*

Morpho peleides *is ready for its first flight*

The birth of Lepidoptera

When the metamorphosis is completed, the pupa bursts open and the butterfly or moth crawls out. At first the wings are small and somewhat rumpled up. The wings of a newborn lepidopter are elastic. The insect looks for a spot where it has the room to develop its wings. It hangs from the empty pupa skin or from a branch and forcefully pumps blood into the veins of its wings. These become bigger and bigger until they have reached their definite measurements. The butterfly or moth then hangs for a few hours to let its wings dry. This causes the wings to lose their elasticity. When they have hardened well, the butterfly or moth pumps the blood back out of its wings. The wings are then strong and light and the butterfly or moth can take flight for the first time. Most butterflies crawl out of the pupae early in the morning. It is not that warm yet and the air is still humid from the dew. Then they have more opportunity to pump up the wings and let them dry than in the middle of the day in the blazing sun. Once the butterfly is able to fly, it goes looking for congeners and the whole cycle starts again from the beginning.

Papilio polymnestor *hangs to dry*

Hypolimnas bolina

3 Lepidoptera and their environment

Lepidoptera make great demands on their living environment.

Temperature, humidity and amount of sunlight are important and they are also dependent in many ways on all kinds of special plant species. Therefore they are a good indication of the quality of the environment. Even if there are small, but still harmful influences in an area, this is quickly seen by changes in the numbers of the different butterfly and moth species in the area.

Lepidoptera and climate

First of all, Lepidoptera need warmth in order to fly. Most of the species prefer a body temperature of 30 to 35 degrees.

Lepidoptera are cold-blooded. This means that their body has the same temperature as its surroundings. So butterflies are highly dependent on the warmth of the sun. To become a little bit active, a minimum temperature of 15 degrees is necessary. Butterflies then crawl out to warm themselves in the sun, using their wings as sun collectors and transporting warmth to the flight muscles.

If it gets too warm, they retreat to a spot in the shade. If they cannot find shade they close their wings above their bodies and turn towards the sun.

In that way, the smallest possible area of the body is warmed by the sun. Moths, too, can only fly with warm muscles. In the evening or night they beat their wings rapidly without taking flight.

All this muscle work provides the neces-

Amauris-*butterfly*

Papilio rumanzovia

Mother of Pearl

Troides rhadamanthus *drinks nectar*

sary energy to warm up the flight muscles, so that they will soon be able to fly.

Lepidoptera, flowers and plants

Most Lepidoptera need nectar from flowers for energy. Flying is an energy-consuming activity. The great majority of the females need such energy for the development of the eggs. Besides nectar, the juices of rotting fruit can also serve as energy source.

Noctuid Moths do not look for flowers at all, but only drink the juice of rotting bananas. Not only dissolved sugars are of vital importance for the butterfly or moth, but water is also indispensable. Many butterflies drink the dew drops found on plants at dawn.

Others come to the riverbank to drink water.

A plant gives the energy-rich nectar to butterflies and other flower-visiting insects as a kind of reward for their help with pollination, which means carrying pollen from one flower to another. The form of a flower is often adapted to a certain group of insects. The characteristic feature of a flower adapted to butterflies and moths is that the nectar can only be reached by the long, thin proboscis of a butterfly or moth. Bumblebees and flies

Papilio machaon, *the Swallowtail*

Caligo *with wings half opened*

Alcon Blue laying eggs

A Geometrid Moth

simply cannot reach it. The flower of the honeysuckle is totally adjusted to pollination by moths, such as Hawk Moths. The white flowers are easy to see in the dusk and also have a lovely scent to attract moths from far and near. The flower releases its lovely scent just when the evening falls. During the day, insects simply do not play any part in the pollination of the honeysuckle. Many butterflies and moths prefer flowers of a certain colour. Hairstreaks, for example, are often found on flowers with a bright red colour.

Female butterflies are extremely picky about the plant species they lay their eggs on. This plant is called a host-plant. Some butterflies only lay their eggs on leaves or other parts of just one plant species: the Cranberry Fritillary, for example, only lays her eggs on the cranberry.

Other butterflies make use of a number of related plant species: the Citrus Hairstreak does not only lay her eggs on

Papilio demoleus *lays eggs on citrus plants*

lemon and orange trees, but can also use other plants of the family of the Rutaceae as host-plants. Among the butterflies and moths there are, or course, species which are not so strict. The leaves of a broad-leaved tree are specific enough for most Atlas Moths.

Butterflies and ants

Any form of Lepidoptera is usually considered to be a victim, the innocent prey, which simply cannot defend itself. A number of butterfly species, all belonging to the family of the Blues, have developed a special relationship exclusively with ants.

The Gentian Blue, the Large Blue and the Scarce Large Blue spend part of their lives in the nests of myrmicinae. As little caterpillars, they are taken by the worker ants to their underground nest.

There the Blue caterpillars fill their stomachs with ant larvae and food that is offered by the ants. The ants are not aggressive towards the caterpillars, because they have organs which secrete a sweet, protein-rich substance. The ants love that.

So the Blues not only see to it that the ants do not consider them as prey, but also that the female worker ants protect them from attacks from parasitic flies and ichneumon wasps. Moreover, during the winter they are underground in the ant nest. There is almost no safer place for caterpillars to overwinter.

A life full of danger

Lepidoptera are threatened by numerous insectivores in practically all stages of their life cycle. For many vertebrates, particularly birds, butterflies, moths and caterpillars are a nutritious and therefore very attractive prey. In the breeding season, when the parent birds have to feed their hungry, screeching young, they carry hundreds of caterpillars to the nest each day.

Bats go after moths, which visit fragrant flowers at twilight to drink nectar and, while flying about, try to find suitable candidates for mating. Bats track down their prey in the dark with the aid of echolocation. They emit high-frequency sounds. If the sounds reverberate against a moth, the bat can locate the prey and immediately grab the victim. If a moth

A crab spider caught a butterfly

Dragonfly, a fierce hunter in the sky

has a densely coated body, the sounds of the bat are smothered in the hairs.

Because no sounds can reverberate, the predator does not know that there is a moth in the neighbourhood and flies on. Some species of moths have special auditory organs in their chest or abdomen. These ears are extra sensitive to the frequency of the bat. If such moths hear only the slightest sound, they drop from

A praying mantis is an insatiable insectivore

Camouflaged moth

Camouflaged moth

Troides rhadamanthus (Golden Ornithoptera) often lays her eggs on the plant next to the host-plant

the sky like a stone, hoping to be too quick for the bat. There even are moths that make a wailing sound which confuses the bat.

The many invertebrates are a much greater threat. Spiders, dragonflies, praying mantis and predatory flies go after the butterflies and moths, while beetles, ants and in particular parasitic wasps make countless victims among the caterpillars.

Digger wasps and ichneumon wasps lay their eggs in or on a caterpillar. When the wasp larvae emerge from the eggs, they start to eat the caterpillar. The horrible part of this is that they do not kill the caterpillar first, but 'eat it to death', as it were.

Sometimes eighty to a hundred little ichneumon wasps crawl out of one caterpillar, and then they all go looking for a new victim.

To withstand this diversity of predators, all forms of butterflies and moths have their special tricks to stay alive.

Vulnerable eggs

To hide the eggs from the view of eggs snatchers, the female usually lays them against the bottom of the leaves of the host-plant. They are glued to the plant with a sort of collagen. This way the eggs are protected from the blazing sun and cannot be washed off the leaf during rain showers. In order to be less noticeable, the eggs of butterflies and moths change colour when they are a few days old. Fresh butterfly or moth eggs are light yel-

The caterpillar, an appreciated prey

A Caligo caterpillar pressed against the vein

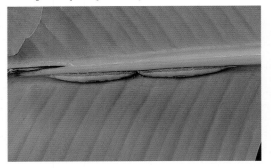

Caterpillar of the Papilio polytes *in a defensive attitude*

low to light green, but they soon become darker and therefore less visible. Plants can react to the presence of eggs on a leaf by letting the leaf fibres die off around the egg.

The leaf becomes mouldy at such spots and this mould also overgrows the eggs. Females of the Golden Ornithoptera therefore lay their eggs on the strong plant which their host-plant, the *Aristolochia*, has wrapped itself around.

Without being bothered by mould, the caterpillars crawl out of the egg after a week and look for the thin, delicate leaves of the *Aristolochia* to fill their stomachs.

Caterpillars

Caterpillars are a much appreciated snack for many insectivores. To escape from all these dangers, caterpillars have a range of tricks at their disposal. Many

Papilio caterpillar

caterpillars have camouflage colours, through which they do not stand out against the background of the plant they are sitting on. Some of them even look like a twig or a withered leaf.

Skipper caterpillars are a good example of this. Hairstreak caterpillars often like bird droppings. Because birds do not eat their own droppings, such a bird dropping exterior is an excellent way to escape from predators. After a Hairstreak caterpillar has sloughed several times, it is too big to pass for a bird dropping.

On the next sloughing it therefore changes from a dropping into a small monster with a blown-up head and striking sham eyes.

When Hairstreak caterpillars are disturbed during their meal, for example by ants, they can drive away these dangerous predators with a so-called osmaterium. This is a forked organ which can be protruded from right behind the head and which spreads a penetrating, deterrent odour.

Pupae and cocoons

Once a caterpillar has become a pupa, it is unable to move. It does not have any wings or legs. This makes the insect very vulnerable. One way to make it through the pupa stage safely is to provide a protecting casing. A hole under the ground is a safe place for the pupae of many Hawk Moths. A cocoon is also a frequently used way of forming a protective casing around the pupa.

The firm cocoon of the Argema mittrei

The pupa of the Dryas julia

Well-camouflaged moth

Some cocoons consists totally of silk thread. This is the case, for instance, for the Emperor Moths and the commercial silkworm (Bombix mori). Other bombycids weave soil, bark or leaves into the cocoon to be camouflaged as far as possible.

Pupae that have to do without a safe cocoon often have a plant-like appearance to avoid being noticed. They bear a striking resemblance, for example, to a shrivelled leaf, a fruit or a broken twig. The colour of the pupa is usually adapted to the surroundings. Pupae are green when they are attached to a leaf and brown when they hang from a twig.

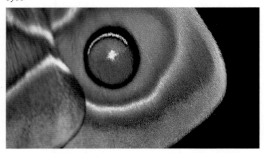

Beautiful camouflage colours

Colours and self-defence

Lepidoptera are a favourite prey for most insectivores, because they are apparently unable to really defend themselves. They do not have jaws to bite with nor a dart to sting with. Yet it is not right to portray Lepidoptera as totally innocent. They can protect themselves in many ways with the colours on their wings. Many Lepidoptera withdraw themselves from enemy sight by using their camouflage colours.

Thanks to those colours, the lepidopter disappears, as it were, into the surroundings. This is true of many moths. As long as they keep still during the day, they will escape the attention of most insectivores.

The tops of the wings of many butterflies are more strikingly coloured and the bottoms have, at first sight, dull colour patterns. If such butterflies suddenly dart between the plants in the event of an emergency, and close their wings above

Attacus atlas with a snake head on the fore-wings

Mother of Pearl

them, they seem to have suddenly disappeared.

The eye-spots are a very familiar pattern on the wings. With those large, striking sham eyes, the lepidopter mimics the head of a large animal, for example an owl. The eyes at the bottom of the hind-wings of Noctuid Moths, sometimes called Owlets, make them look like owls. For small insect-eating birds, that is reason enough to leave such a form alone. Atlas Moths even have a complete snake's head at the tip of each fore-wing to make them look frightening.

In sharp contract to the Lepidoptera with camouflage colours are the butterflies which are coloured bright red or bright yellow.

Such colour patterns are meant to be striking. These butterflies are usually poisonous, or at least distasteful.

Predators that eat such a butterfly become ill. Once they have had such an experience, it is engraved in their memory and in the future they will leave such brightly coloured butterflies alone. These are usually not shy and do not fly away

Dryas julia is brightly coloured on top of the wings

when bothered, but open their wings to let the frightening message of the colours get across even better.

Mimicry

A large number of caterpillars feed on poisonous plants. They store this plant poison in their body and keep it even after pupation when they have become a butterfly or moth. Such poisonous, inedible Lepidoptera almost always have a striking colour pattern on their wings.

If a predator eats such a lepidopter, it

Strikingly coloured butterfly from Thailand

Papilio rumanzovia is not poisonous, but does have the colours of a poisonous butterfly

The strikingly coloured caterpillar of the Danes plexippus, *the Monarch*

Euides isabella *is poisonous*

becomes ill. Upon the next encounter with a lepidopter having the same colour pattern, it will remember the bad experience and will leave the lepidopter alone.

Laboratory tests have shown that after eating one poisonous Monarch Butterfly, jays were deterred by the striking orange and black colour pattern. They remembered the consequences of eating a Monarch even six months later.

After having learned by experience, the birds will leave such a butterfly alone in the future. Other butterflies and moths make use of this. There even are butterflies which are not poisonous or inedible at all, but look like a poisonous type. The edible species are left alone because

Heliconeus is poisonous and looks like the Euides isabella

the colour pattern on the wings brings back bad memories to the birds. This is called mimicry. There is a model and an imitation which appear in the same environment. Sometimes two or more species, which all are inedible, have the same colour pattern on the wings. This serves to strengthen the effect.

In many species of Lepidoptera, only the females are protected by mimicry patterns, possibly to maintain the credibility of the colour pattern. If too many tasty butterflies mimic an inedible model, the effect of the colour patterns will be lost. The result is that great differences can occur between males and females. Even

so great that it only becomes apparent to an expert that two lepidoptera belong to the same species when they mate.

Papilio dardanus

Idea leuconoe is extremely poisonous

Araschnia levana, *the Map Butterfly*

4 Lepidoptera in difficult times

Butterflies and moths from regions with temperate climates are faced with the winter: a period with very low temperatures when there are no flowers, herbs or leaves on the trees. In tropical and subtropical regions there may not be a winter, but there are regular periods of heavy drought, which have a similar adverse effect on the plant growth. In one way or other, butterflies and moths have to survive these periods.

Hibernation and overwintering

To survive such extreme periods of time,

Hibernating Monarchs

butterflies undergo a sort of rest period which is called the diapause. Growth and development then stand totally still and the reserves present in the body are used as efficiently as possible. The stage of the life cycle at which the diapause is undergone differs from species to species. Silver-Studded Blues, for example, overwinter as eggs that are stuck to the woody parts of a heath plant. Caterpillars of the Copper and the Gatekeeper retreat to a clump of shrivelled grass in the autumn, while caterpillars of the White and the Swallowtail pupate just before the winter. In several species the butterflies or moths themselves seek a cool and protected spot in the autumn. The Bromstone, the Peacock and the Small Tortoiseshell are examples of Dutch butterflies which seek a suitable spot in the autumn and hang there motionless for months until spring finally arrives.

Migration

Many European butterflies and moths are born in the Mediterranean region and then migrate to the north as far as Sweden. Similar large distances are covered each by a large number of Painted Ladies, Pale Clouded Yellows and Gamma Moths, to name a few. These insects die in the autumn without providing a generation that survives the winter. Each year, therefore, new butterflies and moths come from warm regions.

Some species of butterflies and moths migrate from certain area to find a place elsewhere to spend the winter. Just like birds, they fly hundreds or even thousands of kilometres to find the right place. They do not go to the really warm places, but to places where the temperature does not drop below freezing. In such conditions their metabolism stands virtually still and they spare the reserves which are stored in their bodies. A similar form of migration has been observed in the Red Admiral.

The most famous migrating butterfly is the North American Monarch Butterfly. The Monarchs appear virtually everywhere in the world, but their migrating behaviour is peculiar to the butterflies which fly from Canada to Central America. After the summer, the butterflies migrate from large parts of the continent over distances of sometimes more than 3000 kilometres to the south. They fly during the day at a speed of 35 kilometres per hour via fixed routes to a few forests in countries including Mexico, precisely to spend the winter there.

Millions of them at a time hang in the trees, crowded together in large bunches. The branches bend under the weight of these gigantic numbers of Monarchs. The climate in these forests is ideal. The

Hibernating Monarchs

Danaus plexippus, a spectacular migrating butterfly

humidity is high, so that the butterflies are not in danger of drying out. The temperature is virtually constant and does not drop below freezing.

It is a safe place to overwinter. In the spring when the plants start growing and blooming again, the Monarchs leave the Mexican forests and make their way to the north. This is where they lay their eggs, from which a new generation of Monarchs emerges.

The butterflies that had survived the winter are no longer alive at that time. During the summer one generation after another appears, going steadily further into North America. Until suddenly, in the autumn, all those butterflies once again migrate south to the same forests where their great grandparents had also spent the winter.

The migration of the Monarchs is and remains an astonishing phenomenon in the world of butterflies.

Danaus plexippus, *the Monarch, overwinters en masse*

5 Observing exotic butterflies

Butterflies and moths have fascinated people for centuries. Collectors travelled around the world looking for these beautiful insects. In the last century complete expeditions were even equipped to enrich collections with new, yet undiscovered species. No means were shunned in those days to collect the insects. If those very first collectors were unable to catch the butterflies in their nets, even bows and arrows or bullets were used to get a special butterfly. Fortunately, nowadays museum collections are not compiled in this way anymore. However, there have always been collectors who have used skilful and responsible methods to catch butterflies for their collection.

This urge to collect has made it possible for many natural history museums to have very extensive collections of prepared butterflies. People who are interested can always go there to admire the enormous wealth in the world of butterflies and other insects.

Part of the collection of the Zoological Museum of the University of Amsterdam

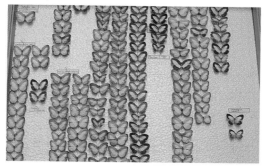

Part of a butterfly collection

Scientific collection

It is possible to see the collection held by the Entomology Department of the Zoological Museum of the University of Amsterdam only by appointment. This collection, containing over 8 million insects, is for the sole purpose of scientific research. This is true of virtually all the zoological and natural history museums in the world. Questions about the ap-

pearance of butterfly species in certain parts of the world, about changes through time in their area of distribution, about variation in form and colour within a species can be answered there after careful research.

As a general rule, the museum keeps everything for scientific purposes. Thus, not only are there collections of native and exotic butterflies and moths, but also valuable collections of other groups of insects, such as flees, lice, beetles, grasshoppers and flies, to name a few.

In this paradise for insect lovers, about 250 butterflies and moths were photographed for this encyclopaedia.

Butterfly gardens

Living exotic butterflies can currently be seen in tropical butterfly gardens. Such gardens offer visitors plenty of opportunities to enjoy these flying jewels. A stroll in such a paradise, where the most beautiful butterflies fly around your head, is an unforgettable experience.

The first butterfly garden was constructed by David Lowe on the Channel Island Guernsey. In a vacant tomato glasshouse, he designed a garden that was as close as possible to the natural habitat of a number of tropical butterflies. Now and then, friends and acquaintances would come and take a look. But interest soon became so great that the glasshouse was opened to the public in 1977. Since

The Tropical Butterfly Garden of the Noorder Dierenpark in Emmen

Watering plants in the Tropical Butterfly Garden

Caligo atreus *smells the alcohol in the cocktail*

then butterfly gardens have been opened not only in England, but also in Malaysia, Florida, Denmark, Luxembourg, France and Germany. They are usually individual attractions. Sometimes, however, as in Emmen, San Diego and Melbourne, they are part of a zoo.

The Tropical Butterfly Garden in the Noorder Dierenpark in Emmen was opened on 30 May 1985. The garden is the largest in Europe and is open all year round. Tropical butterflies flying from flower to flower can also be enjoyed in the winter. To keep up the butterfly population, at least 70 butterflies a day have to emerge from the pupae. Thus, the breeding of butterflies is very important. Pupae are also sent to Emmen from tropical countries by post. In countries such as Costa Rica, the Philippines and Malaysia there are so-called butterfly farms. On such tropical butterfly farms, host-plants are grown first of all for caterpillars. These are bred to pupae, most of which are sold. After a short period of time, butterflies emerge from

The pupae case

Danaus similis

the pupae, and are then set free. In this way the butterfly farms in Belize and Papua New Guinea contribute to the improvement of the butterfly population. An important source of income for such centres is the shipment of large numbers of pupae to butterfly gardens all over the world.

In the Tropical Butterfly Garden of the Noorder Dierenpark, the temperature is at least 25 degrees C. during the day.

This is necessary, because the flight muscles of the butterflies do not work at colder temperatures. If the temperature rises above 28 degrees, the cooling system starts automatically. This is more for the sake of the visitors than the butterflies, which are still quite comfortable at 32 degrees C.

At night the temperature may drop to 20 degrees. The humidity in the butterfly garden remains at a tropical level because of the large amount of water exud-

ed by the plants. The Tropical Butterfly Garden is a colourful greenhouse. Some plants serve to decorate the garden, others are specially for the butterflies, for example the plants whose flowers have to provide the butterflies with nectar. A

Troides *drinks from an artificial flower*

48

large number of these are necessary, because there are as many as 1500 butterflies flying about. There are fewer flowers mainly in the winter because of the shorter days. In order to prevent a shortage of drinking water, the butterflies are able to quench their thirst at about 60 artificial flowers. These consist of four colour combinations drawn on plastic plates. The heart of each artificial flower contains a tube which is filled daily with honey water. Next to some artificial plants there is a tray with rotting fruit, such as bananas or oranges, for the butterflies and moths that do not drink nectar. The butterflies and moths make good use of these artificial flowers, not only in the winter but also during the rest of the year. There are also several host-plants in the garden, specially for the butterflies and moths.

The females have to lay their eggs: passiflora for the Heliconias, citrus and Aristolochia plants for the different species of Hairstreaks, bananas for the Noctuid Moths, cestrum for the Clearwing Butterflies, kalanchoe for Danish Blues and so on. Many butterflies lay their eggs on

Danaus plexippus on the host-plant Asclepias

Caligo memnon, *the noctuid moth, on a rotting banana*

host-plants in the butterfly garden, but there are butterflies that fly around in a large room behind the scenes. It is a few degrees warmer there, and so-called daylight lamps also burn 16 hours a day. Particularly the South American butterflies feel at home in these circumstances and lay large numbers of eggs. The butterfly caretakers bring the plants with eggs to a special breeding room for the caterpillars. There the caterpillars eat large amounts of their favourite plant. When they are finished eating and have pupated, the caretakers harvest large numbers of pupae. The garden service gets back the plants that have been chewed bare. These plants receive special care in a sort of 'rehabilitation greenhouse'.

After a few months they need to have formed enough leaves to fill the always empty stomachs of the caterpillars again. The butterfly pupae, which are fastened to a plant by spun silken threads, are loosened carefully. The caretaker then carefully sticks are needle through the spun thread and is thus able to put the pupae in a special rack. When the rack is full, it goes to the 'emerging cage' in the butterfly garden. There the visitors can witness the birth of a butterfly. When the butterflies are able to fly, the caretaker opens the door and the butterflies can spread their fragile wings for the first time. And so there are tropical butterflies to admire all year round in the Tropical Butterfly Garden in Emmen.

Heteropterus morpheus, *the Large Chequered Skipper*

6 Hesperiidae – Skippers

Skippers are generally small butterflies with thick heads. More than 3500 species are known worldwide.

Most of the representatives of this family live in South America. In contrast to the European species, these Skippers there are brightly coloured and sometimes have tails on their hind-wings.

Skippers have small wings in proportion to their heavy bodies. A wingspan of 30 millimetres is large by European standards, but some tropical Skippers can reach a wingspan of 80 millimetres. When flying, therefore, these butterflies move their wings at a high speed. This makes their flight extremely fast and darting.

The Skippers are also equipped with a remarkably long proboscis. Their antennae can be distinguished from those of other butterflies by the geniculate end. Skippers lay eggs which are spherical to oval and have a flatted base. The hairless caterpillars of the Skippers live in tubes, which they spin by attaching leaves of the host-plant to each other with spun silken thread.

In such a tube they cannot be seen by insectivores. They only leave their house in order to eat.

The caterpillars also use spun threads when they pupate. The pupa is hidden in

Grizzled Skippers and Wood Whites

between the vegetation in a wide-mesh, thin cocoon.

Carcharodus alceae

Carcharodus alcae, the Mallow Skipper, has an area of distribution ranging from northern Africa via Europe to Central Asia. This butterfly likes warmth. It flies in areas with a lot of bare, stony land. When it settles, its wings remain spread. Partly because of its camouflage colours, it is hardly noticeable. The Mallow Skipper drinks nectar from herbaceous plants. They lay their eggs on different species of mallow. The caterpillars grow rapidly. Each year there are two or three generations of this butterfly. The

A skipper

Carcharodus alceae, *the Mallow Skipper*

full-grown caterpillar hibernates in a cocoon. In contrast to most other Skippers, the butterfly flies great distances and colonises many new regions.

Carterocephalus palaemon, *the Chequered Skipper*

Carterocephalus palaemon

Carterocephalus, the Chequered Skipper, is found in the cold and temperate regions of Europe, Asia and North America. The butterflies live in grasslands and swamps on the edge of a wood. Males of the Chequered Skipper sit on a suitable branch and keep an eye on their territory. Females of this Skipper also fly about in a restricted area. Eggs are laid on different species of grass *(Graminae)*. The caterpillars take ten months to grow and develop. In the full-grown stage, the caterpillars hibernate in a tube of spun grasses. In the spring they leave their spun tube and pupate within a period of two weeks. There is only one generation of Chequered Skippers a year.

Erynnis tages

Erynnis tages, the Dingy Skipper, flies in a enormous area of distribution, which covers the whole of Europe and stretches further into China and Eastern Asia. It is a very small, well-camouflaged Skipper. The butterflies prefer cooler regions.

Erynnis tages, *the Dingy Skipper*

There is usually just one and sometimes a small second generation. The Dingy Skipper lays relatively few eggs. The host-plants belong to the family of the Leguminosae. Bird's-foot and Crown vetch are used the most. The caterpillars hibernate in firm cocoons. In the spring they emerge from their safe casing to pupate. The butterflies are home-loving and have very little tendency to extend their area of distribution.

Hesperia comma, *the Silver-Spotted Skipper*

Hesperia comma

Hesperia comma, the Silver-Spotted Skipper, can be recognised by the white comma-shaped spots on the underside of its wings. This Skipper is distributed over an enormous area. It is found in Northern Africa, Europe, Asia and North

America. It likes open forests with bushes and grasses. The butterflies drink a lot of nectar from thistle flowers. They lay their eggs in the autumn on sheep's' fescue and Corynephorus (Graminae). The Silver-Spotted Skipper overwinters as an egg. It is hidden in a tube of grass-stalks, which are spun together. The growth of the caterpillars takes place in the spring and the summer. The butterflies usually fly out in August. They can appear in large numbers in fairly small regions.

Heteropterus morpheus

Heteropterus morpheus, the Large Chequered Skipper, flies from Western and Central Europe to East Asia. The butterfly is restricted to humid areas, such as the transition between forest and high moorland and other swampy areas. The host-plants of the caterpillars are species of grass, of which Molinia and hennengras are favourites. The average growth period of the caterpillars is as long as ten to eleven months. Only in humid areas does the quality of the host-plant remain so long at a high level that the caterpillars can continue eating all that time. Almost full-grown caterpillars hibernate in a tube of spun leaves. There is only one generation each year of this very vulnerable butterfly.

Ochlodes venata, *the Large Skipper*

Ochlodes venata

Ochlodes venata, the Large Skipper, is a commonly found inhabitant of Europe and Asia as far as Japan. It is absent in the northern parts of Scandinavia and the warm regions around the Mediterranean. It has a preference for woody areas. Males of the Large Skipper have a dark striking spot with scent scales on their fore-wings. The eggs are laid on a large variety of grass species (Graminae) and sedges (Cyperacea). The caterpillars grow very slowly. The just hatched caterpillar feeds on wide-leafed grass species for a long time. When it is half grown, it spins a tube of grass stalk in which to hibernate. There is one generation each year, which flies from June to August.

Pyrgus carthami, *the Safflower Skipper*

Pyrgus carthami

Pyrgus carthami, the Safflower Skipper, is a small Skipper that is found from Central Europe to Central Asia. The butterfly is recognisable by the row of white spots along the back edge of the hindwing that look as if they were drawn with a pencil. The Skipper can be found in flowery meadows and roadsides. The host-plant for the caterpillar is mallow or one of the many species of cinquefoil. The caterpillars hibernate in the leaf litter, where they have spun together a number of leaves with spinning thread. After the hibernation the caterpillars grow further and pupate. One generation a year of this butterfly flies in June.

Pyrgus malvae, *the Grizzled Skipper*

Pyrgus malvae

Pyrgus malvae, the Grizzled Skipper, is distributed throughout large regions of Europe and Asia as far as Mongolia. However, the number of Grizzled Skippers is decreasing almost everywhere. This Skipper likes to loiter along the edges of forests, where it stands out by its fast flight, which is regularly interrupted to rest on the ground. The butterfly regularly drinks nectar from the wild strawberry, Ajuga and cinquefoil (Rosaceae). The caterpillars of the Grizzled Skipper eat leaves of the same plant species. When the caterpillar is full-grown, it makes a wide-mesh cocoon in which it hibernates. There is only one generation a year.

Spialia sertorius

Spialia sertorius, the Red Underwing Skipper, is found in northern Africa and almost the whole of Europe. The very small Skipper is recognisable by the red underside of the hind-wings and the red point of the abdomen. The host-plant is the small burnet (Rosaceae). The butterfly can only reproduce when this plant is blooming, because the eggs are only laid on the buds of this plant. The caterpillars eat and grow until after a period of two months they are full-grown. The adult caterpillar then hibernates in an airy house of spun leaves. The pupa is also in a wide-mesh cocoon. The flight-time of the Red Underwing Skipper is from April to June. Sometimes there is a second generation in July-August.

Thymelicus lineola

Thymalicus lineola, the Essex Skipper, is found in northern Africa, Europe, Asia and North America. The closely related *Thymelicus sylvestris,* the Small Skipper, can only be distinguished by the yellow underside of the ends of the antennae. The small Essex Skipper is a fairly common sight in grasslands and at roadsides. The density of butterflies can be very high in such areas. Females of this Skipper lay their eggs in August together

Thymelicus lineola, *the Essex Skipper*

Zela onara

in groups on spikes of grasses. The egg overwinters there. In the spring, when the grass plants develop young sprouts, the caterpillars emerge from the eggs. A large variety of grasses serve as host-

plants for the caterpillars. These are fully grown within two months and pupate. The pupa stage lasts less than three weeks. The butterflies fly in July and August in one generation.

Zela onara

Zela onara is a tropical Skipper from the warm regions of Southeast Asia. The host-plant for the caterpillars of this Skipper is the coconut palm. Other palms are also accepted as host-plant. When the caterpillars are not eating, you can barely see them, because then they sit on the underside of the palm leaves. Moreover, the greenish caterpillars are flattened lengthways against a vein. This Skipper can do a lot of damage to plantations, because a few butterflies are capable of laying large numbers of eggs on the palms.

The presence of the caterpillars is not evident until the damage is already extensive.

Ornithoptera priamus

7 Papilionidae – Ornithoptera

Over 900 species of butterflies belong to the Ornithoptera, or Bird-Winged family. They are large striking flyers. They are also the largest butterflies in the world. Some female Ornithoptera have a wingspan of 25 centimetres. The males are usually a lot smaller, but are more strikingly coloured. Shiny green and gleaming gold decorate their wings. Precisely because of their beautiful colours collectors offer high amounts of money for an intact male, for the rare species even

Papilio inopinatus, *male*

The male of this Ornithoptera shows its green sheen

Papilio inopinatus, *female*

more than 7000 dollars for one single butterfly. International protective measures were therefore necessary to protect these butterflies from extinction.

A great difference in appearance between male and females of a species does not only occur in this Ornithoptera but also in many other Ornithoptera families. Many Ornithoptera have tails on their hind-wings. The ones with dragontails, an extremely small representation of the family, are the most remarkable. Their wingspan is not even 5 centimetres, but the length of their tails can reach 5 centimetres. Other butterflies in this extensive family, such as the Apollo and several Papilionidae butterflies, do not have tails.

The Ornithoptera find their food in flowers, preferably red and purple ones. When they suck up the nectar, they do not sit still, but hang fluttering their wings while drinking. When the butterflies fly about looking for food, they also

Papilio dardanus

57

encounter congeners. When an Ornithoptera male sees a butterfly he suspects to be a female congener, he flies right in front of and under her. During the flight he keeps throwing himself backwards while his wings brush the antennae of the female. With this manoeuvre he emits an aromatic substance to convince the female that they are congeners. If this is indeed the case, such a courtship flight

A mating of the Parides iphidamas

results in mating. Male butterflies of families including the Parides and Troides have a fold in the inner ridge of the hindwings. This fold contains the scent scales, which are white and threadlike.
Female Ornithoptera lay spherical eggs with a smooth surface. Ornithoptera eggs can reach a diameter of 4 millimetres. When laid, the eggs are often yellow, but after a few days they become dark, so that they are less noticeable on the plant. In many Papilionidae, the caterpillars which just emerge from the egg have the

appearance of bird droppings. This provides excellent protection against being devoured by birds, because what bird would search the leaves for food and then eat something that could be its own dropping! The caterpillars grow by sloughing. With the first sloughing a larger bird dropping appears.
The last stage usually has a totally different appearance. The caterpillar is then so big that it does not pass for a bird dropping anymore. These smooth caterpillars have eye-spot markings on the front part of their body. In an emergency they can,

The bird dropping is sloughing

as it were, blow up that part and give predators the impression that they are some kind of frightening lizards or other dangerous animals. For many predators this is reason enough to leave the caterpillars alone. Only insects such as ants do not let themselves be frightened off that easily. To keep these dangerous predatory insects away, the caterpillars

A caterpillar resembles a bird dropping

The caterpillar of the Papilio polytes

protrude an organ which is called an osmaterium. It is right behind the head, is bright orange or yellow-coloured and spreads a penetrating odour which even deters ants. Caterpillars of the so-called Southern Festoon feed on the poisonous Aristolochia plants. They store the poison in their body. This way they make

Papilio caterpillar with bulging osmaterium

A pupa of the Papilio demoleus

called 'belted pupae'. Caterpillars spin a belt with which they fasten themselves to a plant in a characteristic position.

sure that they are inedible, for example for birds. If birds eat such a caterpillar, the plant poison is released in their digestive system. The bird becomes sick for a while. Such caterpillars have fleshy, rose red projections on their bodies, which let birds know that they are inedible. The pupae of Ornithoptera are so-

A Pachliopta caterpillar with striking colours

Allancastria cerisyi

Allancastria cerisyi

Allancastria cerisyi

Allancastria cerisyi lives on mountain slopes in Greece and Turkey. It is at home mainly in rough areas at greater heights. On the stony slopes this special Ornithoptera finds the host-plant of the caterpillar: Aristolochia.

Atrophaneura alcinous

Atrophaneura alcinous, is found in China, Taiwan, Japan. The butterflies fly along the forest edges and in open parts of the rainforest. This is where the host-plant of the caterpillars grows, *Aristolochia tagala* (Aristolochiaceae). The females lay a single egg each time on the youngest leaf on the apical meristem of this climbing plant. Only this way can they compete with the much larger Ornithoptera caterpillars, which are on the large firm leaves of the same plant. The poisonous substances in the plant make the caterpillars and butterflies inedible.

Atrophaneura alcinous

Atrophaneura coon

Atrophaneura hageni

Atrophaneura nox

Atrophaneura coon

Atrophaneura coon, has a very large area of distribution. It is found in the northern region of India, in Burma, Thailand, Laos, Vietnam, Cambodia, the southern region of China, Malaysia and Indonesia. Eight subspecies are distinguished, of which mainly the subspecies from India are very rare. *Atrophaneura coon* is distinguished by its long, thin fore-wings, which are very pronounced in the males. They also have unusually shaped tails on their hind-wings, which break off easily. The bright yellow abdomen is a warning to birds that the butterfly is inedible. The host-plant of this butterfly species is *Apama tomentosa,* a plant of the Aristolociaceae family. The butterflies visit many lantana flowers.

Atrophaneura hageni

Atrophaneura hageni is a rather rare butterfly, whose area of distribution is restricted to the highlands of Sumatra (Indonesia). The butterfly closely resembles the *A. priapus,* which also has a white head. The illustration shows a male with the inner ridges of the hind-wings folded open, so that the white scent scales are visible. The wingspan of this butterfly is 10 to 13.5 centimetres.

Atrophaneura nox

Atrophaneura nox is found in the southern part of Thailand, Malaysia and on a number of islands of Indonesia. Females of this butterfly are almost entirely black with some white along the veins of the wings. Males have a blue sheen on the black of their fore-wings. They also have a yellowish to grey-white band on the inner ridge of the hind-wings, marking the place of the scent scales. The wingspan of the *Atrophaneura nox* is 7.5 to 12 centimetres. The dominant colour of this butterfly is black. To this it owes its name, nox, which means night.

Atrophaneura polyeuctes

Atrophaneura polyeuctes is found in China and Taiwan. The butterflies fly in the open parts of the rainforest. Males visit places with moist sand to drink

Atrophaneura polyeuctes

Atrophaneura polyeuctes

Atrophaneura priapus

The *Atrophaneura priapus* is unique to Java. It is found from sea level to 2000 metres high in the mountains.

It prefers to drink the nectar of lantana flowers. Within the family of *Atrophaneura*, this butterfly species is distinguished by its yellow instead of red warning colours. The colours of the female are much paler than those of the male. The white head is characteristic of a few representatives of the family, which gave rise to the name White Head Batwing for *A. priapus*.

Atrophaneura varuna

Atrophaneura varuna

Atrophaneura varuna has an area of distribution ranging from the north-eastern part of India, Burma, Thailand, Laos and Vietnam to Malaysia. The tails on the hind-wings are absent, as is true of more *Atrophaneuras*. The butterfly is totally black with a few light stripes on the fore-wings. The wingspan of the *A. varuna* is 15 centimetres. It owes its name Batwing to its dark appearance and its size.

water containing dissolved minerals. Females look for *Aristolochia* plants on which to lay their eggs. Research has shown that 50% of the butterfly eggs which are laid on this host-plant are parasitised by ichneumon wasps. The caterpillars and butterflies are inedible. Many butterflies mimic the colour pattern of this poisonous *Atrophaneura* and are therefore left alone by insectivores.

Atrophaneura priapus

Battus philenor

Battus philenor is found from the northern part of the United States to Costa

Battus philenor

Battus polydamas

Rica in Central America. Males and females are much alike. Both sexes have tails on their hind-wings, but the tails of the female are a bit larger. The colours on the hind-wings of the males are a bit brighter and also have a blue sheen. The butterflies visit pink and orange flowers of many plant species to drink nectar. Females lay their eggs on leaves of the poisonous *Aristolochia* plant.

The caterpillars and butterflies are therefore inedible. The appearance of the butterflies is mimicked by many other butterfly species in North America: a beautiful example of mimicry.

tails on the hind-wings. Characteristic is the row of yellow spots along the hind-ridge of this otherwise black butterfly. The colour differences between males and females are minor. Females lay their eggs in groups on leaves of many species of the *Aristolochia* family. The caterpillars stay together in groups and devour the leaves of the poisonous host-plant. The caterpillars and butterflies are therefore poisonous, too, and inedible for birds and other predators. It has been determined that some species of these butterflies live for three months.

Bhutanitis lidderdalei

Battus polydamas

Battus polydamas

Battus polydamas has a large area of distribution. It is found in many parts of North and South America. A large number of geographical forms of this *Battus* species are known. None of them have

Bhutanitis lidderdalei

Bhutanitis lidderdalei is the best known of the four species of this extraordinary butterfly family.

B. mansfieldi and *B. thaidina* are seen very seldom in some provinces of China, while *B. ludlowi* is only found in Bhutan. The area of distribution of the *Bhutani-*

tis lidderdalei ranges from Bhutan, Northern India, Burma and Thailand to the bordering parts of Southern China. In India the butterfly is legally protected. The biggest threat to the preservation of the butterfly is the large-scale cutting down of trees in the forests of Thailand. *Bhutanitis lidderdalei* flies in the wooded areas of the Himalayas at an altitude of 1500 to 3000 metres. When the butterfly is still, it holds its fore-wings over the colourful spots on the hind-wings and then is barely visible. When interrupted, it suddenly shows the bright colours on its hind-wings to frighten its enemy. It then has the opportunity to fly away and is much harder to catch. The caterpillars of the *Bhutanitis lidderdalei* feed on plants of the Aristolochiaceae family.

Chilasa clytia

Chilasa clytia is an Ornithoptera which flies in large parts of Asia. Therefore, many subspecies have been described,

each of which is found in a restricted area. It appears in India, China, Thailand, Malaysia and on many islands of Indonesia and the Philippines. At first, the appearance of the butterflies does not resemble an Ornithoptera, mainly because of the absence of the tails. The caterpillars feed on plants which belong to the Auriantiaceae family.

Cressida cressida

Cressida cressida is the only species of the *Cressida* family. The butterfly is found in New Guinea and in Australia. Normally the males and females fly about slowly, but in an emergency they can bring themselves to safety as quickly as an arrow. Females are generally paler, because they lose many of the pigment-holding scales on their wings rather early. Males are much more brightly coloured and look exactly like the poisonous *Pachliota polydorus*. The *Cressida cressida* itself is also inedible, because

Chilasa clytia

64

Cressida cressida, *female*

Cressida cressida, *male*

the plants on which the caterpillars live belong to the family of the Aristolochiaceae. *Aristolochia pubera* and *A. thozetti* are the most important ones. Both plants grow in open forests in areas along the coast.

Eurytides agesilaus

Eurytides agesilaus is found from Mexi-

Eurytides agesilaus

co and Central America to large parts of South America. It is a relatively small butterfly with a wingspan of 7 or 8 centimetres. Characteristic of the species are the five parallel stripes on the front edge of the fore-wing. A striking red band runs along the black line in the middle of underside of the hind-wing.

Eurytides calliste

Eurytides calliste

Eurytides calliste is found from Mexico to Panama in Central America. It is a resident of humid rainforests on mountain slopes 700 to 800 metres high. This is a rather rare butterfly. Only individual insects are usually observed. In the morning only, males go to the ground to drink at moist places. They also fly about the treetops. They can fly zigzag as fast as an arrow, which makes them difficult to catch. Their wingspan is 9 centimetres.

Eurytides marcellus

Eurytides marcellus is a North American butterfly that lives in forest areas along rivers. The butterfly can fly very fast. The caterpillars feed on plants of the *Annona* and *Asimina* families. The butterflies drink the nectar of the croton and cordia. Only the males drink water from mud pools that form in the forests during the rainy season. A characteristic of *Eurytides* species is that the body is

Eurytides marcellus

Eurytides pausanias

Eurytides pausanias is a rare sight in Costa Rica and Panama. It is also found in small numbers in Columbia, Venezuela, Surinam, northern Brazil, Ecuador, Peru and Bolivia. In many respects, the butterfly resembles *Heliconius wallacei* or *Heliconius cydno*. Its appearance and manner of flying are very similar. But the *Eurytides pausanias* males visit mud pools to drink water and especially dissolved minerals, and a Heliconius does not.

Eurytides philolaus

Eurytides philolaus

The area of distribution of *Euytides philolaus* ranges from Mexico to large parts of Central America. The butterfly is fairly common the year round, but is often present in very large numbers in May and June. The host-plant of the caterpillars is *Sapranthus* (Annonaceae). The caterpillars feed and rest on the leaves. When fully grown, they pupate on the ground between the fallen leaves. The pupa simply lies between leaves. Males and females hardly differ from each other in appearance. However, some females are almost completely black.

very short compared with the size of the wings. The tails of the butterflies of the spring generation are relatively short, but those of the butterflies that fly in the summer are extra long. This how they got their name in the United States: Swordtails.

Eurytides pausanias

Graphium androcles

Graphium androcles is a fairly large representative of the *Graphium* genus. The

Graphium androcles

Graphium codrus

wingspan of this butterfly can reach 9 centimetres. It is found on Sulawesi and the Sula Islands *Graphium androcles* is one of the many butterfly species that are found only on Sulawesi. Such species are called endemic. Despite its restricted area of distribution, it is a common sight and is not considered to be endangered.

Graphium antiphates

There are twelve known subspecies of *Graphium antiphates*, which are specific to parts of the distribution area. This butterfly is found in large regions of India, Sri Lanka, Burma, Southern China, Thailand, Laos, Vietnam, Cambodia, Malaysia and Indonesia. It is a fairly common butterfly in those parts of the rainforests which are not situated at too great a height. The butterfly can be recognised by the five black bands on its forewings. This has given it its English name

Graphium antiphates

Five Band Swordtail. The plants eaten by the *Graphium antiphates* caterpillars come from the Annonaceae family.

Graphium codrus

Graphium codrus is found in the Philippines, New Guinea, Bougainville and the Solomon Islands. There is much variation in the appearance of this butterfly species. The wide band across the forewing can have many colours, varying from pale yellow to green. The band of the males also has a sheen. For the rest, males and females closely resemble each other. *Graphium codrus* always flies round the treetops and only comes down to the ground to drink. This could be nectar from flowers or the juice of rotting fruit, but also water from marshy mud pools.

Graphium doson

Graphium doson appears in India, Sri Lanka, China, Japan, the Philippines, Malaysia and Indonesia. The butterfly closely resembles *Graphium sarpedon* but, unlike this species, has a row of spots along the edges of the wings. Males have striking scent stripes on their wings. It is a quick and nervous flyer. Females lay eggs on plants of the Annonaceae and Lauraceae families, of the latter especially on the *Connamomum* camphor tree. During the day, the caterpillars rest on the tops of the leaves and

Graphium doson

Graphium latreillanus

can hardly be seen. The pupae are placed against the underside of a leaf, and sometimes also on the trunks and branches of neighbouring trees.

Graphium illyris

Graphium illyris is found in the West African countries: from Guinea, Sierra Leone, Liberia, the Ivory Coast Ghana, Togo and Benin to Nigeria, Cameroon, the Congo and Zaire. It is an inhabitant of the low-lying rain forests. The butterfly is distinguished by the long tails on the hind wings and the yellow band across the fore and hind-wings. The wing span varies from 7 to 9 centimetres.

Graphium latreillanus

Graphium latreillanus is found in the western part of Africa from Sierra Leone, Liberia, the Ivory Coast, Ghana, Togo

and Benin to Nigeria, Cameroon, the Congo, Zaire, Uganda and Angola. This butterfly species can be recognised by the light green to yellow spots on the fore and hind-wings and the row of parallel bands along the rear edge of the hind-wings. Its wingspan is 6.5 to 9 centimetres.

Graphium ridleyanus

Graphium ridleyanus appears in large regions of Africa from Sierra Leone in the west to Zambia and Angola. The butterfly is at home in the tropical rainforests in its area of distribution.

Through its characteristic form and the red and black colour pattern, this *Graphium* looks exactly like an *Acrea*, a genus of butterflies which are extremely bad tasting. They strongly resemble an *Acrea* in their appearance as well as in their manner of flying. Together with the

Graphium illyris

Graphium ridleyanus

butterflies which they mimic so well, the *Graphium ridleyanus* males often visit mud pools to drink water. Therefore it is called the Acrea Ornithoptera.

Graphium sarpedon

Graphium sarpedon has a large area of distribution. The butterfly with the striking blue band is found in Korea, Japan, India, Burma, Thailand, the Philippines, Indonesia and Australia. It is at home in forests and open areas. Its favourite nectar comes from lantana flowers. *Graphium sarpedon* is not picky in its choice of host-plant. It chooses among plants from different families, such as Myrtaceae, Sapotacea and Lauraceae. In Australia, it sometimes causes damage to the camphor trees cultivated there.

Graphium weiskei

Graphium weiskei is found in higher regions of New Guinea, in the rainforests at an altitude of 1200 to 2000 metres.

There is little difference in the appearance of males and females. With respect to behaviour, the differences are great. The females are seldom seen, whereas the males fly round the treetops in the morning and search for flowers with nectar they can drink. They also gather on moist sand to drink water and dissolved minerals. They are very wary. If interrupted, they fly away immediately and continue drinking a few metres further up. They seek nectar in the flowers of bushes and low trees.

Graphium weiskei

Graphium sarpedon

Graphium weiskei

Iphiclides podalirius

Iphiclides podalirius, *the Scarce Swallowtail*

Iphiclides podalirius

Iphiclides podalirius, the Swallowtail, is found in the warm and hot regions of Europe and Asia. They prefer hilly areas with warm, dry places where individual bushes grow. Large numbers of males fly together round the hilltops. The caterpillars feed on sloe leaves. They grow fairly rapidly. They are fully grown in a month. They hibernate in the pupa stage. Their flight-time is May and June.

Lamproptera meges

A very special member of the Ornithoptera family is *Lamproptera meges*, a small butterfly that appears in large areas of Southeast Asia, particularly Burma, Malaysia, Indonesia and the Philippines. Its only relative is *Lamproptera curius* which, unlike Lamproptera meges, has a white band across its wings. This unusual butterfly can be found in sunny, open places in forests on the banks of swiftly flowing rivers and streams. It is rather small for an Ornithoptera. Its wingspan is not even 5 centimetres. The tails of these butterflies are extremely long Part of the fore-wing is translucent. The butterfly has a dancing flight with an enormously rapid wingbeats. When flying, it gives the impression of a dragonfly. Only when it settles does it become clear that

Lamproptera meges

Ornithoptera alexandra, *male*

it is a butterfly. The wings of the butterfly continue to beat even when it is still. The caterpillars feed on plants of the Combretaceae family.

Ornithoptera alexandrae

Ornithoptera alexandrae is the largest butterfly in the world. Females of this

Ornithoptera alexandrae, *female*

Bird-Winged butterfly can have a wingspan of 28 centimetres.

The distribution of this butterfly is restricted to small parts of the rainforest in the Popondetta Valley on Papua New Guinea. This is mainly a result of the limited availability of the only plant on which the female will lay her eggs, *Aristolochia dielsiana*.

The unique aspect of this is that, while the females are extremely critical regarding the choice of the host-plant, the caterpillars are much less so.

Research has shown that the caterpillars can be successfully relocated to other species of *Aristolochia* plants.

The development from egg to butterfly generally takes more than four months. The butterflies themselves can attain an age of three months. This butterfly has few natural enemies.

However, the laying of plantations with oil palms, cacao trees and rubber trees is a very big threat. Numerous measures have been taken to save this spectacular butterfly species from extinction: on the one hand, a legal ban on catching and possessing the butterfly; on the other hand, planting the host-plant in neighbouring areas and introducing this butterfly in remote regions where *Aristolochia dielsiana* also grows. The most important of all is preservation of the forests in which *Ornithoptera alexandrae* is still found.

Ornithoptera chimaera, female

Ornithoptera chimaera, *male*

Ornithoptera chimaera

Ornithoptera chimaera is found in New Guinea and Java.

It prefers to live in rainforests at an altitude of 1200 to 1800 metres. The size of the butterfly varies considerably in both sexes. The wingspan of the males varies from 7 to 15 centimetres, and that of the female from 8 to 18 centimetres. The butterfly is a powerful flyer that, gliding and then diving, searches for flowers such as those of hibiscus plants.

At the altitude where *Ornithoptera chimaera* flies, the host-plant, *Aristolochea momandul*, has thick, sturdy leaves. That is why small caterpillars feed on the top and the young leaves, and the larger caterpillars eat the older leaves. The host-plant grows abundantly along rivers and streams.

Ornithoptera croesus, *male*

Ornithoptera croesus

Ornithoptera croesus is a very endangered Bird-Winged butterfly, which is only found on a few islands of the Moluccas. The butterfly lives in forests in the lowlands with swamps and other tropical biotopes which are not easily accessible. Nevertheless, they are endangered, because in precisely the same places the most precious trees grow that can be cut in the rainforest. Insecticides are often sprayed in the swamps to kill the mosquitoes, with of course disastrous consequences for this splendid butterfly. Females can reach a wingspan of almost 20 centimetres, while the males come no further than 15 centimetres. The butterfly was first collected and described in the last century by Alfred Russel Wallace, a contemporary of Charles Darwin. The shining, gold-coloured wings of the Bird-Winged butterfly inspired him to write the following:

Ornithoptera croesus, female

"When I took the butterfly out of the net and folded open its magnificent wings, my heart began to beat heavily, blood rose to my head. I felt more of a tendency to faint than if I had been confronted with death itself."

Ornithoptera goliath

Ornithoptera goliath is at home on New

Ornithoptera goliath *in New Guinea*

Caterpillar of Ornithoptera goliath

Ornithoptera goliath, *male*

Ornithoptera paradisea, *male*

Ornithoptera goliath, *female*

Ornithoptera paradisea, female

Guinea and the Moluccas. It lives in tropical rainforests in mountainous regions at an altitude of 500 to 1500 metres. The wingspan of a female can be as much as 21 centimetres. *Ornithoptera goliath* is therefore the second-largest butterfly. *Ornithoptera alexandrae* is actually the largest, with a wingspan of 28 centimetres. However, *Ornithoptera goliath*, does hold the record for the 'largest butterfly egg', its egg having a diameter of 4.7 millimetres. Goliath eggs are laid on *Aristolochia* plants. The growth of *Ornithoptera* caterpillars proceeds rather slowly and can even take longer than two months.

Ornithoptera paradisea

Ornithoptera paradisea is a beautiful Bird-Winged butterfly which is distributed in small populations in the northern part of Papua New Guinea. The male has

tails on his hind-wings that are characteristic of the species. Both males and females prefer to fly round the treetops in forests on mountain slopes and in valleys. The host-plant of the caterpillars is a rare plant species in the Aristolociaceae family. The egg stage lasts almost two weeks, the caterpillar stage six or seven weeks. The pupa stage also lasts longer than six weeks. The butterflies live about three months. They do not fly long distances, but remain in a fairly restricted area. *O. paradisea* is one of the few butterfly species for which worldwide protective measures are in force.

Ornithoptera priamus

Ornithoptera priamus appears in many different forms in Australia, New Guinea and Indonesia. There are four subspecies in Australia, and ten on the surrounding islands. The males of the subspecies have

Ornithoptera priamus *caterpillar that has just sloughed*

Ornithoptera priamus, *pupa*

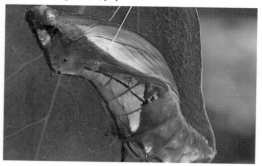

Ornithoptera priamus, *butterfly*

Ornithoptera priamus, female

Ornithoptera priamus, *caterpillar*

different wing colours. These can vary from orange, blue and green to gold-coloured. The wingspan of the males is about 14 centimetres. They sail round the treetops, as it were, and only fly further down in the rainforest to drink nectar from the red flowers of the lantana and hibiscus. Females regularly fly low to the ground when they are searching for plants on which to lay their eggs. The host-plant for the caterpillars is Aristolochia. The Ornithoptera females often lay their eggs on neighbouring plants. It appears that many eggs are parasitised by tiny wasps. If the butterfly egg is not on the host-plant, but on the plant next to it, it is much more difficult for the wasp to find. The caterpillars eat the eggshell first and then go on to devour the host-plant at a rapid pace until it is bare. In spite of their large size, they can be fully grown within 14 days. They sometimes cannibalise smaller caterpillars. They

Ornithoptera priamus urvillianus

Ornithoptera rothschildi, *female*

sometimes also pupate on neighbouring plants, especially after the host-plant has been eaten bare.

ORNITHOPTERA PRIAMUS URVILLIANUS

This is a striking blue subspecies that is found on Bougainville, the Bismarck Islands and the Solomon Islands.

Ornithoptera rothschildi

The distribution of *Ornithoptera roth-schildi* is restricted to the Arfak mountains in the north-western part of New Guinea. Although this butterfly is found in a relatively small area, it is not considered to be an endangered species. In some places there are many examples of this species flying about. The butterfly is a great favourite of collectors, but does not enjoy legal protection in Indonesia, in contrast to many other *Ornithoptera*

species. *O. rothschildi* looks a bit like *O. goliath*, but the green iridescent colours on the fore-wings of the males are not as bright. *O. rothschildi* is also somewhat smaller. The wingspan of a female is not more than 15 centimetres. The butterflies are at home in the mountains at an altitude of 1800 to 2400 metres. They can be found in ravines and valleys, where they are protected from the strong wind. This area is extremely inaccessible. The result is, on the one hand, that little is known about this butterfly. On the other hand, the living environment of *O. rothschildi* is not attractive to the wood industry.

As long as its biotope is not threatened, this Bird-Winged butterfly will not be endangered.

Ornithoptera tithonus

Ornithoptera tithonus has an area of distribution which is restricted to the

Ornithoptera rothschildi, *male*

Ornithoptera tithonus, *female*

western part of Irian Jaya and a few neighbouring islands, such as Walgeo, Misool and Salawati. It is a relatively large representative of the *Ornithoptera* genus, as females can have a wingspan of 22 centimetres. The males usually do not exceed 16 centimetres. *Ornithoptera tithonus* lives in the forests on mountain slopes, but is observed occasionally at sea level. Although *O. chimaera* has a preference for the same areas in New Guinea, both sorts are not found together. *O. tithonus* is probably the last remnant of a butterfly species that once had a much wider area of distribution. For this reason, the butterfly is also very vulnerable and falls under legal protection measures in Indonesia. It is still an *Ornithoptera* for which much further research will be necessary in order to find out what ecological conditions are important for the survival of this butterfly species.

Ornithoptera victoriae

Ornithoptera victoriae is widely distributed over the Solomon Islands, an island group to the east of New Guinea. The females, which can reach a wingspan of 18 centimetres, have yellow colours on their wings in addition to black and white. The males are much more colourful, thanks to their striking green, yellow and orange iridescent colours. The butterfly has been named after Queen Victo-

Ornithoptera tithonus, *male*

Ornithoptera victoriae, *female*

Ornithoptera victoriae, *male*

ria. The first example was shot for her in mid-air in the mid 19th century. Even now, the butterfly is desired by collectors to such an extent that legal protection is necessary. Nevertheless, agricultural activities, which have caused many natural living environments to disappear, are the greatest threat to this butterfly.

Pachliopta aristolochiae

Pachliopta aristolochiae is found in China, Burma, Laos, Cambodia, Vietnam, Malaysia and Indonesia. Their host-plant is the poisonous *Aristolochia tagala* (Aristolochiaceae). The colour of the caterpillars varies from pinkish grey to black. The caterpillar absorbs poisonous substances from the plant. These make the caterpillar and the butterfly inedible for insectivores. The striking red colours of their body and the red and white colour pattern on the wings are a

Pachliopta aristolochiae

warning that the butterflies are poisonous. Males and females of this species are almost identical in appearance.

The colour pattern of *Pachliopta aristolochiae* is mimicked by numerous butterfly species. Thousands of them at once go to places where they spend the night together.

Pachliopta hector

The area of distribution of *Pachliopta hector* is restricted to Sri Lanka and the southern and eastern parts of India. These butterflies are legally protected in India, although the species is not considered to be endangered. The host-plants of the caterpillars are plants from the Aristolochiaceae family. The orange and red spots on the top and underside of the wings are a warning that these butterflies are inedible. This species serves as a model for one of the types of *Papilio*

Pachliopta hector

polytes females. *Pachliopta hector* is found at sea level as well as in mountainous areas up to an altitude of over 25000 metres. The butterflies enjoy the nectar of lantana flowers. At night they gather in large numbers at common sleeping places.

Pachliopta kotzebuae

Pachliopta kotzebuea

Pachliopta kotzebuea appears on a few islands of the Philippines. Five subspecies are known. This *Pachliopta* species has no white spots at all. The red spots and red body colour indicate that the butterfly is inedible, at least for vertebrate insectivores, as spiders and ants, for example do not seem to be deterred. The butterfly flies mostly along the forest edges where it goes looking for its host-plant Aristolochia.

Pachliopta polydorus

Pachliopta polydorus is found from Indonesia, New Guinea and many other island groups, such as the Solomon Islands, to Australia. As a result of the diversity and the size of this area of distribution, at least 31 subspecies of this *Pachliopta* are known. *Pachliopta polydorus* is not a fast flier. It stays along the edges of the rainforest. *Aristolochia tagala* and *A. thozetti* are the host-plants of the caterpillars. Within 14 days, the

Pachliopta polydorus, *underside*

Pachliopta polydorus, *underside*

Papilio aegeus, *male*

Papilio aegeus, *male*

caterpillars are full-grown and pupate. The pupa hangs on the host-plant and is beautifully camouflaged as a seed or fruit. After three weeks, the butterfly emerges, which is striking mainly because of the red warning colours of the thorax and abdomen. Many biologists classify *Pachliopta* and *Atrophaneura* as the same genus, which used to be called Polydorus.

Papilio aegeus

Papilio aegeus is a common butterfly in New Guinea and Australia. These Ornithoptera also visit the parks and gardens of the cities. They are good flyers that can fly away at lightening speed when disturbed. Their host-plants are microcitrus, halfordia, micromelium and other plants from the Rutaceae family. They can sometimes cause damage to citrus plants in orchards. The colour of the pupa depends on the place where the caterpillar pupates. On leaves and green stems it is green, on older branches it is greyish brown. The *Papilio aegeus* males are the same in the entire area of distrib-

Papilio aegeus, *female*

Papilio aegeus, *vrouwtje*

Papilio aegeus

Papilio agestor

The females lay their eggs on the leaves of the machilus, a plant from the Lauraceae family.

Papilio ambrax

Papilio ambrax is found on some Indonesian islands, on New Guinea and in the north-eastern region of Australia. It flies from sea level to an altitude of 1200 metres in mountainous regions. The host-plants of the caterpillars are micromelum, euodia, zanthoxylum and clausena, all plants from the Rutaceae family. The caterpillars can also be found in orchards where citrus trees are grown. Male and females drink a lot of nectar from stachy-tarpeta flowers. Only the *Papilio ambrax* females look exactly like *Pachlioptera polydorus*, not just in appearance but also in behaviour. A female *P. ambrax* normally flies about very calmly. Like the males, they only shoot away when dis-

ution. There are different form of females, particularly in New Guinea.
These female Ornithoptera resemble different species of poisonous butterflies that fly in the same area, and are therefore avoided by birds.

Papilio agestor

Papilio agestor is found in the northern part of India, Burma, Thailand, China, Vietnam, Laos and Malaysia. The butterfly does not look at all like an Ornithoptera, but is an exact copy of *Danaus sita*, a light brown and inedible species of Monarch butterfly. The manner of flying and the position of the wings when the butterfly is at rest are exactly like those of the Monarch butterfly. The wingspan of this butterfly species is 8 to 9.5 centimetres. *Papilio agestor* males patrol their territory, chasing away intruders and courting females of their species.

Papilio ambrax

Papilio ambrax

Papilio anchisiades

turbed. A real *P. polydorus* never tries to escape from enemies in that way, but keeps on flying calmly, relying on its warning colours.

Papilio anactus

Papilio anactus is a common sight all year round in the eastern part of Australia. It can also be seen in southern Australia from October to April. The butterflies always fly in sunny places. The host-plants of the caterpillars are *Eremocitrus glauca* and *Microcitrus australis* (Rutaceae). In addition to these native Australian plants, they also feed on cultivated citrus. The total life cycle of the butterflies, which fly in the summer, lasts about two months. Caterpillars that emerge in March and April hibernate as pupae. The colour of the pupa is determined by the background to which they are fastened. With its wingspan of

Papilio anactus

about 6 centimetres, *Papilio anactus* is a small representative of the *Papilio* genus.

Papilio anchisiades

Papilio anchisiades is found from Texas and Mexico in North America to Brazil. The butterfly has no preference for specific territories. Large numbers of them inhabit a great variety of natural areas. The eggs are laid on casimiroa, zanthoxylum and citrus. The caterpillars all eat at the same time and also slough in synchronously. When the caterpillars are not eating, the gather together in large numbers on the stem of the host-plant. The colour of the pupa varies and depends on the background colour. The butterflies are black with red spots on their hindwings and sometimes white on their forewings. This appearance mimics the females of the poisonous *Parides* species.

Papilio andraemon

Papilio andraemon is found only on Cuba, the Bahamas and the Cayman Islands. The most common *Papilio* species inhabits Cuba. In Jamaica, where the butterfly was introduced, it is a pest on citrus plantations. On Cuba, this Ornithoptera is not a pest, because it has natural enemies which keep their numbers under control. The wingspan is 8 to 10 centimetres.

Papilio androgeus

Papilio androgeus is a butterfly found from Mexico to Peru and Brazil. The eggs are deposited on zanthoxylum and also occasionally on citrus. The green eggs change colour after being laid and become bright yellow. There is a huge difference between the appearance of the male and the female butterflies. The males are yellow and black and have tails on their hind-wings. The females, on the other hand, are dark-coloured and have a green iridescence. This colour pattern makes them look like inedible butterflies. It is not known whether this is due to mimicry or whether the butterfly itself is inedible.

Papilio antimachus

Papilio antimachus is at home in tropical Africa. It is found from the rain-

forests from the west coast of Sierra Leone to Uganda. *Papilio antimachus* is the largest African butterfly. It can reach a wingspan of as much as 23 centimetres. The form of the female resembles that of the male, but is considerably smaller. Males sometimes fly together in groups to find nectar in flowers of blooming bushes or water from mud pools.

Females never allow themselves to be seen in open areas of the forest, but fly mainly round the treetops. The butterfly is not found in large numbers anywhere in its wide area of distribution. It is considered to be rare because it appears almost exclusively in undisturbed rain-forests. Trees are being felled massively in many of the African forests. Measures to protect the butterflies have only been taken in Ghana, the Ivory Coast and Zaire. Because they are extremely poisonous, the butterflies have very few problems with natural enemies.

Papilio androgeus, *female*

Papilio arcturus

Papilio arcturus is found in the northern part of India and in Burma and China. It lives in forests on mountain slopes in the Himalayas at an altitude of 1500 to 3500 metres. It prefers cold to temperate areas, in contrast to *Papilio paris*, an Ornithoptera that closely resembles *P. arcturus* but inhabits tropical regions. *Papilio arcturus* has an 11 to 13 centimetre wingspan. The butter-

Papilio arcturus

Papilio bianor

flies are attracted to the flowers of the hibiscus and lantana; the caterpillars can be found on plants from the Rutaceae family.

Papilio ascolius

Papilio ascolius is found in Central and South America from Costa Rica to Columbia. It is a fairly rare inhabitant of the tropical rainforests at an altitude of about 1000 metres. Males fly about the tops of the tallest trees in the forest, while the females prefer the forest edges along paths and streams. The wingspan is 12 to 13 centimetres. In spite of its large size, *Papilio ascolius* is a beautiful imitation of a *Lycorea*, a genus of poisonous butterflies from the Danaidae family. Females of this Ornithoptera also have the same slow, unusual manner of flying as their poisonous model.

Papilio bianor

Papilio bianor is found in India, Burma, China, Korea and Japan. The butterfly has even been observed in the Himalayas at an altitude of more than 2000 metres. The host-plants of the caterpillars are members of the Rutaceae family. The wingspan varies from 8.5 to 13 centimetres. They have long tails. In the sunlight, both the males and females of *Papilio bianor* have a green iridescent sheen on the tops of their wings.

Papilio cresphontes

Papilio cresphontes is found from the southern United States and Mexico to Central America. This butterfly species is difficult to distinguish from *Papilio thoas*. The form of the exterior sex organs of the males is different and a different host-plant is preferred. *P. thoas*

Papilio ascolius

Papilio cresphontes

Papilio cresphontes

lays its eggs on piperaceous plants. *P. cresphontes* is much less choosy. Plants from the Lauraceae and Solanaceae families are sometimes used as host-plants. The butterflies appear in large numbers in the rainy season. In addition to drinking a lot of nectar from a great diversity of flowers, they also drink the juices from fresh manure.

Papilio dardanus

Papilio dardanus

Large numbers of *Papilio dardanus* are found in many different forms from Equatorial Africa to South Africa.
The males are the same in the entire area of distribution: a rather large yellowish white Ornithoptera with long tails.
The females look the same only in Ethiopia.
Elsewhere, *P. dardanus* females mimic other, poisonous butterflies that fly in the same area. More than a hundred different forms of these are known.

Mating of Papilio dardanus

84

Papilio dardanus, *female*

Papilio dardanus hippocoon

Papilio dardanus, *male*

mate. Female Ornithoptera like to remain within the protection of the forests, while the males of their species fly along the forest edges and paths in full sunlight. The host-plants of the caterpillars are teclea, clausena and citrus (Rutaceae).

Papilio delalandei

Papilio delalandei is unique to Madagascar. Little is known about this Ornithoptera in its young stage and about the requirements set by the butterfly on its environment. It is an inhabitant of the forests in the eastern part of Madagascar. Although the flora and fauna of this island are generally endangered, this butterfly can be seen regularly in large numbers. It has a wingspan of 9 centimetres. The butterfly can be recognised straight-away by the striking green spots at the front edge of the fore-wings. The row of yellow spots in the centre of the fore-wings continue along the hind-wings.

Papilio delalandei

PAPILIO DARDANUS HIPPOCOON

This is one example. This subspecies looks exactly like a butterfly of the Amaurus genus, a group of inedible butterflies from the Danaidae family. The differences in appearance between both sexes are often so great that it only becomes evident that two butterflies belong to the same species when they

Papilio demodocus

Papilio demodocus

Papilio demodocus is found in the tropical regions of Central America, South Africa and Madagascar. The butterfly lays eggs on plants from the Rutaceae and Umbelliferae families. Caterpillars that live on citrus (Rutaceae) have a totally different colour to those living on plants from the other group. This insect can be a pest especially in southern regions of Africa where much citrus is cultivated. Because the butterfly flies in large numbers precisely at Christmas time, it is called the 'Christmas butterfly'.

Papilio demoleus

Papilio demoleus is found in Afghanistan, Burma, China, Indonesia, the Philippines

Papilio demoleus

Papilio demoleus

and Australia. This butterfly is not always appreciated in its area of distribution. The caterpillars can really be a pest on citrus plantations. They do a lot of damage because of their enormous appetites. In Australia, the caterpillars also eat the leaves of different species of *Psoralea* (Fabaceae). *Papilio demoleus* travels great distances there. It is a fast flyer that flies about a metre above the ground and is usually searching for flowers.

Papilio fuscus

Papilio fuscus

Papilio fuscus is found mainly on the Malaysian peninsula and in the north of Australia, as well as on an especially large number of islands lying in between, such as Sulawesi, the Moluccas, New Guinea, the Aru and the Solomon Islands. There are 23 known subspecies of this butterfly, each specific to a certain island. In Australia, the caterpillars feed on microcitrus, halfordia, zanthoxylum, micromelum and citrus flowers in nurseries. These are all plants from the Rutaceae family.

The butterflies spend their time looking for nectar in the flowers of blooming bushes, but also drink water with dissolved minerals from sandbanks.

Papilio garamas

Papilio garamas

The area of distribution of *Papilio garamas* is only from Panama to Mexico. The wingspan is 12 centimetres for the males and 15 centimetres for the females. The males fly in the morning hours round the treetops and seldom come down to the

Papilio glaucus, *yellow form*

ground. Only in the afternoon do they visit flowers such as the *Fuchsia arborea*. They also go to mud pools to drink water containing dissolved minerals. The butterfly appears rarely in collections, because it can usually stay out of the collector's reach. Papilio garamas is not a rare sight in natural surroundings.

Papilio glaucus

Papilio glaucus

This remarkably large Ornithoptera appears in all of North America. There are two clearly different forms of this species. In the northern part of their area of distribution, the males and females have yellow wings with black stripes. This has resulted in the name 'Tiger Swallowtail'. Much further south, there are much darker and even black examples of females. These butterflies mimic the poisonous *Battus philenor*. Female butterflies are not very picky regarding the choice of the host-plant. Beautifully camouflaged caterpillars can be found on poplar, cherry, willow and ash trees. In addition to visiting flowers rich in nectar, the butterflies also drink water from mud puddles and even suck juices from dead animals.

Papilio helenus

Papilio helenus is found in Japan, India, Thailand, Burma, Malaysia and Indone-

Papilio glaucus, *black form*

sia. With a wingspan of 13 centimetres, it is one of the larger Ornithoptera of the *Papilio* genus. The top of the butterfly is completely black with a light green sheen. When it flies, the large white spots under the fore-wings can be seen. When the insect is still, these spots remain hidden under the fore-wings. When disturbed, the butterfly pulls up its fore-wings and suddenly displays the white eye-spots. This can confuse a predator and give the butterfly the chance to fly away. *Papilio helenus* lays its eggs on plants from the Rutaceae family which grow in the forests.

Papilio hesperus

Papilio hesperus is found on the Ivory

Papilio helenus

Papilio hesperus

sary. The butterfly is only found in undisturbed rainforests at not higher than 600 metres. There the males and females visit the flowers of the blechnium, asclepias and lantana. The host-plants of the caterpillars are *Hernandia catalpaefolia* for the eastern and *Hernandia troyiana* for the western population. With a wingspan of almost 15 centimetres, it is the largest of the American Ornithoptera.

Coast, Ghana, Togo, Benin, Nigeria, Cameroon, Sudan, the Congo, Zaire, Uganda, Tanzania and Zambia. It is an inhabitant of the lowland forests in those countries. The wingspan is from 10 to 12.5 centimetres. The yellow colour on the wings can vary from bright yellow with orange to very pale yellow. It is usually only the males of these Ornithoptera which are seen. The *Papilio hesperus* females seldom or never leave the forests where they live.

Papilio homerus

Papilio homerus only appears in two small areas on the island of Jamaica. In both places, the butterfly population is dwindling because the original forests are being cut down to make room for coffee plantations. *Papilio homerus* is officially listed as an endangered species for which protective measures are neces-

Papilio homerus

Papilio jordani

The area of distribution of *Papilio jordani* is restricted to two places on the Minahassa peninsula in the northern part of Sulawesi in Indonesia. The males and females differ considerably in appearance. The male has a wingspan of about 7.5 centimetres and is black with a row of white dots across its wings. The female is not only larger, with a wingspan of 8.5 centimetres, but also has

Papilio jordani, *female*

Papilio jordani, *male*

white with black markings that look exactly like *Idea blanchardi*, a poisonous, inedible butterfly from the Danaidae family. The female has the same manner of flying as an *Idea*, namely an extremely slow wingbeat. In emergencies, it can shoot away just like a real *Papilio*. The butterflies fly all year round, with peaks in November and February. They lay their eggs on plants from the Rutaceae family. *Papilio jordani* is considered to be extremely rare. The peninsula where they are found is very densely populated. Much forest area is being cleared to make way for rice fields. In cooperation with the World Wide Fund for Nature, a national park was established in 1980. The purpose is to secure the flow of water to the rice fields, which could triple the rice production and preserve the vital forests on the mountain slopes.

Papilio karna

Papilio karna

Papilio karna has an area of distribution stretching from the eastern part of Malaysia to many islands of Indonesia and the Philippines.
Although the butterfly is seldom seen and never flies in large numbers, it is not considered as an endangered species. *Papilio karna* males gather at drinking places along riverbanks and the females stay in the rainforests.
The butterfly is striking because of the beautiful green iridescent colours on its

hind-wings, which sometimes have eye-spots.

Papilio laglaizei

Papilio lagaizei

Papilio laglaizei is only found on New Guinea and a few neighbouring islands. It has a wingspan of 7.5 to 9 centimetres. This Ornithoptera looks exactly like *Alcides agathyrsus*, an inedible moth from the Uraniidae family which is active during the daytime. Both species of Lepidoptera often fly together round the tree-tops. The remarkable thing is that there are usually more *Papilio* butterflies present than *Alcides* moths. Thus, *Papilio laglaizei* itself is most likely inedible as well. The bright orange and black caterpillars feed on *Litsea irianensis* and species of cinnamon (Lauraceae). Because both the butterfly and the moth are inedible, this is considered an example of Müller's mimicry: two inedible Lepidoptera look very much alike, which strengthens the effect of their warning colours.

Papilio lowi

Papilio lowi is a fairly large Ornithoptera which is only found on the Philippine island of Palawan and the Indonesian island of Borneo. Despite its small area of distribution, the butterfly is not endangered. The females are very seldom seen, whereas the males fly around freely. Their host-plant is the citrus (Rutaceae).

Papilio lowi

Papilio lycophron

Papilio lycophron

Papilio lycophron is a resident of tropical South America, particularly Brazil. The males are black and have a wide yellow band across their wings. A row of yellow spots runs along the edges of the winds. Their female congeners are dark-coloured and have a green sheen on their wings. Citrus and other Rutaceae plants are their host-plants. These Ornithoptera can do a lot of damage on plantations where grapefruits and oranges are grown.

Papilio machaon

Papilio machaon, the Swallowtail, has an extremely large area of distribution including the northern part of Africa, Europe, Asia and the northern part of North America.

The striking, fast-flying Ornithoptera is found in grasslands and swamps, where host-plants can be found.

The eggs are laid on plants belonging to the Umbelliferae family. Wild carrots, angelica and fennel are its particular

Papilio machaon

91

The caterpillar of Papilio machaon, *the Swallowtail*

Papilio memnon

Papilio memnon.

favourites. Some females lay more than 500 eggs. In many areas there are two generations. The pupa hibernates. Pupae of the summer generation are often fastened to herbaceous plants, while pupae that hibernate are fastened to woody plants.

Papilio macilentus

Papilio macilentus

Papilio macilentus is an Ornithoptera which is striking because of the unusually long tails on its hind-wings. It is found in Japan, Korea and China. It is now a rare butterfly in Korea. The host plant of this butterfly's caterpillars is citrus.

Papilio memnon

Papilio memnon has an area of distribution ranging from India, Burma, China, Malaysia and Indonesia to Japan. There are 13 known subspecies of this Ornithoptera, which usually have a wingspan of about 15 centimetres.

Papilio memnon males not only look different from the females, they also have a very different lifestyle.

The males fly in open areas, while the females stay in wooded surroundings. Some females of this large Ornithoptera species have striking tails on their hind-wings.

The caterpillar lives on plants of the Rutaceae family, to which the citrus also belong.

Papilio nephelus

Papilio nephelus

Papilio nephelus is found in an area reaching from Burma, Thailand, Cambodia, Malaysia and Indonesia to China and Taiwan. Many subspecies of this butterfly are known. Its English name, Banded Helen, refers to its resemblance to *Papilio helenus*, Red Helen.

Papilio nireus

Papilio nireus

Papilio nireus is a butterfly native to the tropical and subtropical regions of Africa. A number of types are distinguished that have a blue-green band across the fore and hind-wings. When sunlight falls on the band, it has a beautiful blue iridescence. The males only have a striking white band on the underside of their hind-wings. *Papilio nireus* flies in both dry regions and rainforests. Several different plants from the Rutaceae family serve as host-plants.

Papilio nobilis

Papilio nobilis

Papilio nobilis is commonly found in Sudan, Kenya, Uganda, Burundi, Ruanda, Zaire and Tanzania. It is an inhabitant of the highland forests up to an altitude of about 2500 metres. On the one hand, this butterfly has the characteristic form of an Ornithoptera, and on the other hand a particularly pale yellow colour, with hardly if any markings. The host-plant of this Ornithoptera's caterpillars is wahlenbergia.

Papilio ophidicephalus

Papilio ophidicephalus is found in Kenya, Tanzania, Zaire, Malawi, Zambia, Zimbabwe and South Africa. It is a

Papilio ophidicephalus

Papilio palamedes, *top*

fairly common butterfly, with ten know subspecies in the different parts of its area of distribution. The long tails on the hind-wings and the striking eye-spots are typical of this butterfly species. Males and females have the same appearance, although the females are somewhat larger. The wingspan is 9 to 13.5 centimetres. The butterflies are active the whole year round in open spaces in the rainforests. The caterpillars of *Papilio ophidicephalus* feed on citrus and other plants belonging to the Rutaceae family.

nectar from a wide range of flowers. Females lay their eggs on plants from the *Persea* genus and other plants from the Lauraceae family. The avocado is often one of its favourite host-plants.

Papilio palamedes, *underside*

Papilio palinurus

Papilio palamedes

Papilio palamedes is a large, dark Ornithoptera that is native to the United States. It prefers to live in swamp areas with a lot of trees. The butterflies like to drink from mud pools. They get their

Papilio palinurus

Papilio palinurus is found in Burma, Malaysia, Indonesia and the Philippines. It is one of the few green butterflies. Green would otherwise seem to be an excellent camouflage colour.

The striking green iridescent band is in sharp contrast to the dull brownish grey underside. *Papilio palinurus* flies in mountainous regions.

Only in Malaysia is it a locally endangered species.

Papilio paradoxa

Papilio paradoxa

Papilio paradoxa has an area of distribution ranging from the northern part of India, Burma, Thailand, Laos, Cambodia and Indonesia to the Philippines.

Despite the enormous area of distribution and the large number of subspecies, there are only two separate colour forms of this Ornithoptera. Both are a copy of a butterfly of the *Euploea* genus. Butterflies of that genus are inedible. *Papilio paradoxa* mimics their appearance, including the blue sheen on the wings. Its behaviour is even identical. Except that when they ae disturbed, they interrupt their slow *Euploea*-like flight and bring themselves to safety lightening fast like a real *Papilio*.

Papilio paris

Papilio paris

Papilio paris is found in the lower regions of India, Burma, Thailand, Laos,

Malaysia and Indonesia and the mountainous regions of China. The blue metallic eye-spots on the hind-wings are intended to confuse enemies.

They give the impression that the insect is the head of an animal. This is how they deter enemies.

Papilio peranthus

Papilio peranthus

Papilio peranthus is found on a large number of islands in the Indonesian archipelago. Little more is known about this Ornithoptera.

Papilio phorcas anorgei

Papilio phorcas

Papilio phorcas is a fairly common phenomenon in the forests of tropical Africa south of the Sahara. Six subspecies have been described, which differ in the size and colour of the pattern of green spots

Papilio phorcas phorbanta

Papilio polymnestor, *male*

Papilio polymnestor, *female*

on the fore and hind-wings. The length of the tails on the hind-wings can also vary considerably. There are two colour forms of *Papilio phorcasm* females. One resembles the males, the other is dark brown with yellow spots. This is a relatively small Ornithoptera in the tropics, with a wingspan of 8 to 10 centimetres. Both males and females visit the flowers of herbaceous and low bushes. The caterpillars eat the leaves of plants of the *Teclea* genus (Rutaceae).

Papilio pilumnus

Papilio pilumnus

Papilio pilemnus is found only in Mexico and Guatemala. This butterfly is a striking sight with its bright yellow colours and long tails on its hind-wings. Nevertheless, little is known about this butterfly. It is not considered as an endangered species.

Papilio polymnestor

Papilio polymnestor is seen regularly in Sri Lanka and the southern part of India. It flies in forests as well as in open areas. It also visits parks and gardens in villages and cities. Neither of the sexes of these Ornithoptera has tails on its wings. The wing span of this large butterfly is as much as 13 centimetres. Males have characteristic silver grey markings on the top of the wings. The markings of the female are usually paler and often more or less yellow-coloured. On Sri Lanka, *Papilio polymnestor* is a migratory butterfly, which regularly flies great distances. The host-plants of the caterpillars are plants from the Rutaceae family.

Papilio polytes

Papilio polytes is found in Southeast Asia from India to China and Indonesia. Many different forms of this Ornithop-

Papilio polytes, *female*

tera are known. Not just the males are different from the females with respect to the colour and form of their wings, but there are also considerable differences in appearance between the females from different parts of their area of distribution. In the northern part of this enormous area of distribution, the species hibernates. The pupa must be able to withstand the winter cold. The caterpillars of this butterfly feed exclusively on plants belonging the citrus family (Rutaceae). The colour of the pupa depends on the background colour. A caterpillar that pupates on a leaf has a green pupa. If it pupates on the trunk of a tree, the pupa is brown. The insect is thus perfectly camouflaged and can undergo its metamorphosis in safety.

Papilio polyxenes

Papilio polyxenes appears in Canada and North and Central America up to the Amazon area in South America. It is

Papilio polyxenes

Papilio polytes

a species of butterfly that has disappeared rapidly on a local level, but which just as easily takes possession of new areas with the right conditions. Males are territorial and occupy the top of a hill. That is where female Ornithoptera come to look for a male congener. Both sexes avoid the shade and fly in full sunlight, looking for flowers. The host-plants are *Apium* (Apiaceae) and *Foeniculum* (umbellifera). *Papilio polyxenes* lays a single egg each time on a seedling. If only larger plants are available, she lays several eggs on each plant.

A *mating of* Papilio rumanzovia

Papilio rumanzovia, *female*

Papilio rex

Papilio rex

Papilio rex is an inhabitant of the higher forests in Nigeria, Cameroon, Sudan, Ethiopia, the Congo, Zaire, Uganda and Kenya. Seven subspecies of this 'royal papilio' are known. The wingspan of this Ornithoptera can reach as much as 14 centimetres. It is identical in colour and markings to the poisonous *Danaus formosa* butterfly. *Papilio rex* is, however, much bigger than the butterfly species whose appearance and behaviour it mimics. It is a commonly appearing butterfly in its area of distribution.

Papilio rumanzovia

Papilio rumanzovia is a large, striking Ornithoptera native to the Philippines. The males and females of *Papilio rumanzovia* differ clearly in colour. There is one

form of males of this butterfly species, while the females can be found in numerous forms having either wide red bands or a striking red-and-white spotted pattern on the tops of their wings. Both sexes have striking red warning colours on the underside of their wings. They try to frighten off enemies with these colours. They have to do this in a convincing manner, because this butterfly species is decidedly not inedible for an insectivore. It only mimics a butterfly that is indeed poisonous.

Papilio rumanzovia, *female*

Papilio thaiwanus

Papilio ulysses

Papilio thaiwanus

Papilio thaiwanus is a large Ornithoptera that, as its name indicates, can only
be found on Taiwan. Despite such a
restricted area of distribution, the butterfly is not considered to be an endangered
species. Little more is known about the
life of this Ornithoptera.

Papilio torquatus, *male*

Papilio torquatus

Papilio torquatus has an area of distribution stretching from Mexico to Bolivia.
The female butterflies lay their eggs on
citrus plants. The seek these plants no
higher than about 800 metres above sea
level. Males fly at a high speed along the
forest edges and open areas of the forest.
In the morning they drink nectar first
and later in the day they go looking for
sandy riverbanks to drink water containing dissolved minerals.
Females remain in the shady parts of the
forest.

Papilio ulysses

Papilio ulysses is found on New Guinea,
the Moluccas, the Solomon Islands and
in Australia. It is a typical rainforest butterfly. When it flies along the forest edge
over a river, the reflections of the beautiful blue wings can be seen from a great
distance. Both sexes have these beautiful
iridescent colours. *Papilio ulysses* males
react very strongly to shining blue.
Sometimes as many as ten butterflies fly
after each other. The males drink water
with dissolved minerals from wet sand.
The butterflies drink a lot of nectar from
lantana flowers. They lay eggs on different species of *Eudoia* (Rutaceae).

Papilio xuthus

Papilio xuthus is found in Japan, Korea
and China. This Ornithoptera looks a lot

Papilio xuthus

Papilio zalmoxis

Papilio zalmoxis

like the *Papilio machaon* Swallowtail. An important difference is the black colour on the wing veins of *P. xuthus*. The host-plant of the caterpillars is poncirus and several other plants of the Rutaceae family. This is one of the most common butterflies in Japan, especially in the summer months.

Papilio zagreus

Papilio zagreus

Papilio zalmoxis is a striking butterfly from the tropical forests of Africa. This 'giant blue Ornithoptera' is found in countries such as Liberia, the Ivory Coast, Ghana, Cameroon, Nigeria, Gabon, the Congo and Zaire. The tops of the fore and hind-wings are vivid blue, in contrast to the underside which is light grey. The colour of the body is bright yellow. The wingspan of the females is not more than 15 centimetres, and that of the man is as much as 17 centimetres. Although the males in particular are often caught, this special Ornithoptera is not known as an endangered species.

Papilio iphidamas

Papilio iphidamas is found from Mexico to Peru. All *Parides* species have a black body with red dots. The basic

Parides iphidamas

Papilio zagreus is a South American butterfly found in the tropical regions of Colombia, Venezuela, Ecuador, Peru and Bolivia. The orange, yellow and black colour pattern of the butterfly, which has a wingspan of less than 12 centimetres, resembles that of a poisonous butterfly from the Heliconiidae or Ithomiidae family. The similarity is so great that the butterfly no longer looks anything like an Ornithoptera. It is a beautiful example of mimicry.

colour of the wings is also black. Males can be recognised by the folded inner edge of the hind-wings. The fold contains white, threadlike scent scales. During courtship, the female remains still on a plant, while the male flies directly above her and dives constantly towards her. During such a dive, the antennae of the female come in contact with the scent scales of the male. The threads can sometimes be seen when the butterflies mate. The females of the various *Parides* species particularly resemble one another. The species can best be distinguished by the red and sometimes green spots on the fore-wings of the males. The host-

Parides iphidamas

plant is the poisonous Aristolochia. The inedible and brightly coloured caterpillar is characterised by white, fleshy protrusions on its body. The butterflies prefer wooded areas and are not rare. The females can be found mainly along the forest edges and in open spaces in the forest, because that is precisely where the host-plants are located.

Caterpillar of parides iphidamas

Parides photinus

Parides photinus flies from Mexico to

Parides photinus

Costa Rica. The butterfly distinguishes itself in appearance by the double row of red spots on the hind-wings. The wings also have a beautiful blue sheen. Males fly about in groups in places where many flowers, especially lantana, can be found and they try to chase each other away. Females visit such places in the morning to display and mate. After mating, the male gives off a substance in the female's sexual orifice. This substance hardens and prevents the female from mating with another male for some time. After the mating, the female spends an almost solitary life. She is constantly searching for young leaves on fresh Aristolochia plants. She lays only one egg and flies away to the next plant. That is why females are found in a much larger area than the males of this butterfly species.

Parnassius phoebus

Parnassius phoebus

Parnassius phoebus is found in mountainous areas in large regions of the northern hemisphere. Their area of distribution ranges from France, Switzerland and Austria via Kazakhstan, Siberia, China and Kamchatka to the western United States and Canada. There are 45 known subspecies of this butterfly, which differ from each other in the number and size of red dots on the wings. *Parnassius phoebus* is a relatively small Apollo butterfly. Its wingspan varies from 5.5 to 6 centimetres. The butterflies fly in mountain meadows at an

Parnassius phoebus

altitude of 1500 metres and higher. They lay their eggs on plants such as sedum, saxifrage and sempervivum.

The egg overwinters. The butterfly is not considered to be endangered on a world wide level, but in the Alps it has become so rare that legal protection measures have been taken.

Pharmacophagus antenor

Pharmacophagus antenor

Pharmacophagus antenor is a large Ornithoptera with a wingspan of 13.5 centimetres which is only found on Madagascar. There have been no known reports from the African continent. Some biologists classify the butterfly under the genus *Parides*, and others under the *Atrophaneura*. Just like the butterflies from that genus, the *Pharmacophagus antenor's* striking red colours on its body and wings are a warning that it is inedible. The caterpillars' host-plants are

Pharmacophagus antenor

Teinopalpus imperialis, *male*

members of the Combretaceae family. Significant numbers of this large Ornithoptera species can still be found on Madagascar, although very many of them are caught for sale to tourists.

Teinopalpus imperialis, *female*

Teinopalpus imperialis

Of the three species of butterflies that belong to the genus *Teinopalpus*, T.imperialis is the most well known. *T. aureus* and *T. behludinii* from the southern part of China are so rare that they are only known from museum specimens. *Teinopalpus imperialis* is scattered throughout the north of India, Nepal, Bhutan, Burma and the south of China. It is a very rare phenomenon, which prefers to fly in the dense forests at an altitude of 2000 to 3500 metres.
It can be seen only in the morning on sunny days in open spaces where males come to drink water with dissolved minerals from mud pools.

The butterflies are never seen on flowers. The females have a wingspan of 12 centimetres and are considerably larger than the males.
The colours of both sexes also differ considerably; to such an extent that they used to be considered to be representatives of two different species.
Males defend their territory against congeners. The best places for this are mountain peaks surrounded by forests. The males chase each other round the mountain peaks.
The host-plant of *Teinopapus imperialis* is a daphne species (Thymeleaceae), a bush that grows in the underbrush of oak forests. The caterpillars pupate at the end of September and then hibernate. The first butterflies can be seen in May, the last still in July. In India there is sometimes a second generation. The biggest threat to this butterfly is the

Newly emerged Trogonoptera

Trogonoptera brookiana

increasing deforestation, which is causing the plant to disappear. For the time being, measures are only being taken in Nepal to protect the forests.

Trogonoptera brookiana

Trogonoptera brookiana is a very striking phenomenon in Malaysia and Indonesia. The wingspan of this Ornithoptera is more than 15 centimetres. Females can

Trogonoptera brookiana, *male*

Trogonoptera brookiana, *female*

be recognised by the white spot on the tip of the fore-wings and the row of white spots along the edge of the hind-wings. The males drink water from mud or rocks along riverbanks. *T. brookiana* females, which fly mostly above 750 metres, lay their eggs on Aristolochia. Although this Ornithoptera is not immediately in danger of extinction, protective measures have been taken nevertheless, as each year many tens of thousands of butterflies of this species are used in pictures to be sold to tourists. *Trogonoptera trojana,*

Trogonoptera trojana, *male*

Troides haliphron

Trogonoptera trojana, *female*

Related species such as Troides socrates and Troides iris can hardly be distinguished from this butterfly.

Troides helena

Troides helena has an area of distribution stretching from Sri Lanka, India, Burma, Thailand, Vietnam and Malaysia to New Guinea. At least seventeen different subspecies have been described. The most important difference in appearance between the males and the females of this butterfly are the row of black dots in the golden yellow field on the female's hindwings. *Troides helena* prefers to fly high, also when it flies in villages and cities. It is the most common Ornithoptera.

an Ornithoptera that looks a lot like *T. brookiana*, is at home on Palawan, one of the Philippine islands. The most important differences in appearance between these two species are the much smaller green band across the hind-wings of *T. trojana*, the much shorter 'tongues' on the fore-wings and the blue iridescent spots on the male's hind-wings.

Troides hypolitus

Troides hypolitus is found on Sulawesi

Troides haliphron

Troides haliphron is found on several islands of the Indonesian archipelago, of which Sulawesi, Sumba, Sumbawa and Flores are the most important. This Bird-Winged butterfly is not known to be rare or endangered, but is nevertheless protected by legal measures taken by the Indonesian government.
At least nine subspecies of *Troides haliphron* are known, which are all specific to the island on which they appear.

Troides hypolitus

and a large number of the Moluccan islands. It is the largest representative of the *Troides* genus. The female's wingspan can reach more than 20 centimetres. The male is characterised by red and black colours on its abdomen, whereas the female has a yellowish tint. The caterpillars feed on plants from the Aristolochia genus. The poisonous substances of this host-plant are stored in their bodies, which makes them inedible for insectivores. The striking golden yellow colours on the hind-wings of a *Troides* are a warning for this.

Troides oblongomaculatus

Troides oblongomaculatus is found from sea level to an altitude of 800 metres in large regions of Indonesia and New Guinea. It can be can be found wherever its host-plant *Aristolochia tagala* (Aristolochiaceae) grows. Males and females of this butterfly species are practically identical. The males can be recognised by the folded edges of their hind-wings, which contain the scent scales. They search for newly emerged females to mate with even before they are able to

Troides oblongomaculatus

Troides oblongomaculatus

fly. These large golden butterflies are attracted by red hibiscus flowers to drink their nectar.

Troides rhadamanthus

Troides rhadamanthus is a 'Golden Ornithoptera' which is at home on the various islands of the Philippines. The yellow tops of the hind-wings sometimes have a beautiful violet iridescent colour. The caterpillars' host plant is *Aristolochia tagala* (Aristolochiaceae). In contrast to most *Ornithoptera*, the *Troides* Ornithoptera are not immediately threatened with extinction. Nevertheless, the same protective measure have been taken for both groups of butterflies.

Zerinthia polyxena

Zerinthia polyxena, the Southern Festoon, inhabits the rocky regions of Southern and Central Europe. The host-plants of the caterpillars are different species of Aristolochia, such as the birthwort. It hibernates as a pupa. This extremely vulnerable butterfly has its flight-time in April and May. There is one generation a year. The Southern Festoon is a striking butterfly with black and yellow markings. The females are considerably larger than the males.

Troides rhadamanthus

Zerinthia polyxena

Delias eucharis

8 Pieridae – Whites

The Whites family contains more than two thousand species, with a great diversity of colours in spite of their name. Many Whites are anything but white. Yellow and orange are the colours of very many Whites.

The English name butterfly is an abbreviation of 'butter-coloured fly', which refers to the Bromstone.

In many cases, White are the most common butterflies in a certain region. In the Netherlands, too, the most common butterflies are the various Cabbage White Butterflies, which appear in great numbers.

A White of the genus Pareronia

The eggs of Whites are reel-shaped and usually white or yellowish in colour. The emerging caterpillars are smooth. In many cases they feed together in large numbers and completely defoliate their host-plant. Before pupating, the spin a belt around themselves in order to fasten themselves to a stem. The pupae always look like some part of a plant, such as a leaf, flower or bud.

Male and female butterflies visit flowers to drink nectar. Hundreds of males only gather together at sandy or muddy riverbanks to drink water containing dissolved minerals. These are mainly the fresh-coloured, undamaged and there-

A migratory butterfly of the genus Colias

fore newly emerged male Whites. They need a certain quantity of minerals to make the pheromones used in courting female Whites.

Different species of Whites, particularly members of the genera *Pieris* and *Colias*, tend to exhibit migratory behaviour. It is not clear why they do this.

Anteos clorinde

Anthocharis cardamines, *a male Orange Tip*

The Anthocharis cardamines *caterpillar*

Anteos clorinde

Anteos clorinde is found from the southern part of the United States, in Texas and Arizona, via Central America to Brazil. The caterpillar's host-plant is *Senna spectabilis. Anteos clorinde* males have a striking yellow spot on the upper edge of their fore-wing. They also have yellow-edged spots in the middle of the fore and hind-wings.

Anthocharis cardamines, *a female Orange Tip*

Anthocharis cardamines

Anthocharis cardamines, the Orange Tip, is found in Europe and the temperate regions of Asia. The caterpillars feed on lady's-smock *(Cardamine pratensis)* and garlic mustard *(Alliaria petiolata)* (Cruciferae). The butterfly owes its name to the striking orange spots on the tips of the male's fore-wings. The caterpillars grow

fast in the early summer. That is when the host-plant flowers and bears unripe fruit. These parts of the plant are eaten by the caterpillars. The Orange Tip hibernates as a pupa. The pupa stage sometimes lasts almost a year. There is one generation a year. The flight-time is April and May.

Aporia crataegi

Aporia crataegi, the Black-Veined White, is found in North Africa, Europe and Asia. It is a striking butterfly with black veins on the almost transparent wings. The host-plants are hawthorn *(Crataegus)* and sloe *(Prunus)*. The caterpillars live together in large numbers in a cocoon. They eat and grow during the summer and hibernate together in the cocoon. When the host-plant has come into bud in the spring, the caterpillars can continue growing. Each year there is only one generation. The butterflies, which only live for one or two

Appias epaphia, *female*

Aporia crataegi, *the Black-Veined White*

Appias epaphia, *male*

Appias nero

weeks, fly in June and July. They have a preference for forest edges.

Appias epaphia

Appias epaphia is one of the few African representatives of this genus, which is otherwise found mainly in Southeast Asia and Australia. This butterfly is a common sight in the tropical regions and sometimes migrates in large numbers. It suddenly appears en masse in a region and disappears just as suddenly. It is a rela-

tively small *Appias* with a wingspan of less than 5 centimetres. The males are almost completely white, with a dark edge only at the tip of the fore-wings. Females have wide black bands along the wings. The host-plants of the caterpillars are different species of capparis (Capparidaceae).

Appias nero

Appias nero is a very common butterfly from India to Burma and Malaysia and on many islands of the Philippines and Indonesia. The bright orange butterfly has a wingspan of 7 centimetres. The tips of the fore-wings are strikingly pointed. Males often gather on the sandy banks of rivers that flow through the forests. The females stay in the forest and often fly round the treetops. The plants eaten by the caterpillars are members of the Capparidaceae family.

Catopsilia florella

Appias pandione

Appias pandione

Appias pandione is found in India, Pakistan, Burma, Thailand and Indonesia. The flight-time of this butterfly is from February to May in regions at an altitude of up to 2000. Males and females are fast flyers which are difficult to approach. The females have more black on their wings than the males. Because both sexes are less black in dry periods, different forms of this species are known. *Appias pandione* has a wingspan of 5.5 to 8 centimetres.

Catopsilia florella

Catopsilia florella has an area of distribution ranging from Africa to China and Malaysia in Eastern Asia. The males are white and have a striking black spot in the middle of their fore-wing; the colour of the females varies from white to yellow. The caterpillars' host-plant is cassia

(Leguminosae). In the African part of its area of distribution, *Catopsilia florella* is a migratory butterfly.

Catopsilia pomona

Catopsilia pomona is found in India, Pakistan and large regions of Southeast Asia, in Australia and also on Madagascar and Mauritius. Migratory flights of thousands of these butterflies can be seen regularly in various parts of the area of distribution. In Australia, this Catopsilia is called the Lemon Migrant. The host-plant of the caterpillars are plants of the cassia genus (Leguminosae). When the caterpillars are at rest, they are pressed against the main nerve of a leaf and are especially difficult to find. In the summer, the caterpillars grow so fast that they are full-grown in only two weeks. The butterfly has a wingspan of 6.5 to 7 centimetres.

Catopsilia pomona

Catopsilia scylla, *wings spread*

Catopsilia scylla

Catopsilia appear in all parts of the world, but particularly in the tropical regions of Southeast Asia. *Catopsilia scylla* lives in Thailand, Malaysia and on the Moluccas. The top of the fore-wings is white with a black edge, while the hind-wings are yellow. On the underside, the fore and hind-wings are yellow with a few brown spots. The host-plant is cassia (Leguminosae).

Colias electo

Colias electo

Colias electo is an African representative of a genus of butterflies which are found almost exclusively in the northern hemisphere.

It is a fairly common butterfly in Africa, and lives mainly in open grasslands at higher altitudes.

The underside of the wings is yellow, the top orange with a wide black band along the outer edge of the fore and hind-wings. The butterfly has a wingspan of 5.5 centimetres.

Catopsilia scylla, *wings closed*

Colias hyale, *the Pale Clouded Yellow*

Colias hyale *mating*

Colias hyale

Colias hyale, the Pale Clouded Yellow, is found in the temperate and warmer regions of Europe and Asia. The males of this butterfly species are vivid yellow, the females pale yellow. The butterflies always rest with their wings closed above their bodies. Therefore, this butterfly can be distinguished from *Colias crocea*, which is orange, when it flies and shows the tops of its wings. *Colias hyale* flies and migrates often, searching for places where its host-plant grows. The eggs are laid mainly on alfalfa, Crown vetch, and clover. There are usually two generations a year. The caterpillars grow during in the late summer. They hibernate as immature caterpillars and grow further

after the winter. It takes about eight months to develop fully. The second generation of caterpillars takes less than a month to grow.

Delias belladonna, *top*

Delias belladonna

Delias belladonna is an almost 'black-and-white' butterfly that is commonly found in India, Pakistan, China, Burma and Indonesia. It flies in mountainous regions up to an altitude of 3000 metres. The butterfly visits many flowers, such as buddleia which are rich in nectar. It is active as from April. In some parts of its area of distribution there are three generations a year.

Delias belladonna has a typical slow manner of flying, which turns into a flight quick as an arrow in the event of danger. It can be recognised by the striking yellow spot at the base of the hindwing. This spot is visible on the top and

Delias belladonna, *underside*

Delias descombesi, *underside*

Delias descombesi, *top*

underside of the wing. The wingspan is 7 to 9 centimetres.

Delias descombesi

Delias descombesi has an area of distribution ranging from India and Pakistan via Southeast Asia to Indonesia. It flies in warm valleys at the foot of the Himalayas up to an altitude of 1500 metres. The butterfly is active in the period from March to December and it visits many flowers. The wingspan is 6.5 to 9 centimetres. The top of the wings is mostly white, while the underside of the hind-wings is vivid orange with two striking red spots.

Delias eucharis

Delias eucharis, a White with a striking, brightly coloured underside, is at home on Sri Lanka and in India, Burma, Malaysia, the Philippines, New Guinea and Australia. The butterflies lay their eggs on the leaves of the mistletoe (Loranthaceae), a parasitic plant. It is the only plant accepted by the caterpillars as food. Great numbers of the caterpillars live together in a large cocoon made of silken thread which they have spun themselves.

Delias henningia

Delias henningia

Delias henningia is a mostly black-coloured White which is at home in the Philippines. It is a butterfly with a vary varied colour pattern. The males of this species come together in large numbers in marshy places to suck up water containing dissolved minerals. The caterpillars feed on plants from the Loranthaceae family. The live happily together in a large cocoon. They are constantly spinning thread. If a caterpillar falls off a branch, it has a kind of lifeline along which it can crawl back into the cocoon.

Delias mysis, *underside*

Delias mysis, *top*

Delias mysis

Delias mysis is found on New Guinea and in Australia. It is a butterfly with many local colour variations. It lives in rainforests and is active all year round as a butterfly. Mainly in the morning hours, it visits lantana flowers and also many flowers of flowering trees in the rainforest. The host-plants of Delias mysis are viscum and other plants of the Lorantaceae family, which live as parasites on citrus plants. The caterpillars live together in great numbers. The pupate on the leaves of the host-plant. Even then, they stay close to each other and sometimes there are 3 or 4 pupae on one leaf. The pupa stage lasts 2 to 6 weeks.

Delias ninus

Delias ninus

Delias ninus is the most common species of Delias in Malaysia and Indonesia. They are strong flyers that visit many flowers in the morning hours. The butterfly has a wingspan of 6 to 7.5 centimetres. The striking thick black bands around the veins of the fore-wings give the butterfly a dark appearance. The red spots at the base of the hind-wing can be seen in various Delias species.

Delias thysbe

Delias thysbe

Delias thysbe is found in Nepal, India, Burma, Malaysia and Indonesia. There are many variations in its appearance. In parts of its area of distribution, for example, it closely resembles Delias ninus. It prefers to fly in sunny places. When the sun goes behind a cloud for a moment, the butterfly rests. The caterpillars live in numbers of 50 to 60 in a large, common cocoon with which they cover the host-plant. They eat plants from the Loranthaceae family.

Dismorphia amphione, *female*

Dismorphia amphione, *male*

Dismorphia amphione

Dismorphia amphione is found from Mexico to the southern part of Brazil. Males have striking white to silver spots on the front part of their hind-wings. Females do not have these spots. The wingspan of the males is 7 centimetres and that of the females 8 centimetres. The colours of the females are particularly reminiscent of butterflies from the Heliconiidae and Ithomiidae families. Because they look like such poisonous butterflies, insectivores leave them alone. *Dismorphia* is the first butterfly for which this type of mimicry was determined. *Dismorphia amphione* flies from sea level to an altitude of over 1000 metres. It is a relatively rare butterfly which prefers to fly along the forest edges. The female lays eggs on plants from the Inga genus, such as *Inga sapindoides* and *I. densiflora* (Mimosaceae). They lay one egg on each leaf. Some caterpillars eat only the fresh leaves, others only the old leaves of the host plant.

Gonepteryx rhamni, *the Bromstone*

Gonepteryx rhamni

Gonepteryx rhamni, the Bromstone, lives in both the cold and warm regions of Northern Africa, Europe and Asia as far as Japan. It is a roaming butterfly that often flies in the neighbourhood of forests where its host-plants, buckthorn and alder buckthorn, can be found. There is one generation a year. The Bromstone hibernates as a butterfly. That is why this butterfly species can live for more than a year. Egg laying time begins at the end of

117

April. Bromstones lay as many as 500 eggs.

Hebomoia glaucippe

Hebomoia glaucippe is found in Japan, and China, and from India and Pakistan to Malaysia. With a wingspan of 10 centimetres, it is the largest of the Asian Whites. The colour patterns of the males and females differ considerably. Males

Ixias marianne

Hebomoia glaucippe, *male*

have bright orange tips on their forewings, females have a lot of black on their fore and hind-wings. Both sexes also exhibit different behaviour. The females only fly in wooded areas, the males are also seen in open territory. The host-plants of the caterpillars are capparis (Caparidaceae). Each year there are two generations of *Hebomoia glaucippe*. The butterflies that fly in the rainy season are usually larger than congeners that fly in the dry period.

Ixias marianne

The area of distribution of *Ixias marianne* is restricted to India, Pakistan and Sri Lanka. With a wingspan of about 5 centimetres, it is a small Orange Tip, characterised by the wide, dark stripes along the edges of the fore and hindwings. The butterflies like sunny places, where they fly about at high speed and suddenly land on a flower or on the wet ground to drink water. *Ixias marianne* females fly low over the ground between bushes and flowering herbs.

Leptidia sinapis, *the Wood White*

Leptidia sinapis

Leptidia sinapis, the Wood White, is found from Western Europe to Central Asia. It is a small White that prefers to stay in the neighbourhood of woods. The host-plants of the caterpillars are field lathyrus, bird's-foot and crown vetch. The pupa overwinters on a strong branch. There are two generations each year. The Wood White is a vulnerable species. It has no tendency to migrate and is therefore dependent on favourable circumstances in its area of distribution.

Pereute charops

Pereute charops is found from Mexico to Peru. Butterflies of the genus *Pereute* are dark-coloured Whites which are the American counterpart of the *Delias* species in Asia. *Pereute charops* is an

Pereute charops

inhabitant of mountainous areas at an altitude of 1200 to 2200 metres. The butterfly has an unusual manner of flying, with moments of rapid wingbeats followed by gliding. The males are territorial. In the morning hours, they defend small, sunlit places in the rain forest. Male congeners who happen to fly by are chased away. In the afternoon, the females begin to deposit their eggs on plants from the Loranthaceae family. They lay their eggs in heaps against the underside of the leaf. The caterpillars live happily together on the host-plant. The pupa of *Pereute charops* looks exactly like a bird dropping and is therefore not likely to be recognised as a tasty bite for an insectivore.

Pieris brassicae

Pieris brassicae, the Large Cabbage White, is found in Europe, Western and

Caterpillars of the Large Cabbage White

Pieris napi, *the Green-Veined White*

Pieris brassicae, *the Large Cabbage White*

Pieris napi

Pieris napi, the Green-Veined White, is found in Northern Africa, Europe, the northern part of Asia and in North America. The butterfly likes warm areas, not only in warm but sometimes also in cold regions. The host-plants of the caterpillars are cabbage species, watercress, meadow cress and mustard garlic (Cruciferae). The caterpillars grow rapidly and pupate within fourteen days. The pupa is also the stage that hibernates. The pupa is fastened to a strong branch, a tree trunk or a stone. There are two, sometimes three generations a year. The Green-Veined White is a very common butterfly that also exhibits migratory behaviour.

Pieris rapae

Pieris rapae, the Small White or Small Cabbage White, is found in the northern part of Africa, Europe, Asia, Australia and North America. It is the most com-

Central Asia and South America. The butterflies lay their eggs in groups on the underside of Cruciferae leaves. Because cabbage plants also belong to this family, Large Cabbage Whites can sometimes be a pest in vegetable gardens.

Other host-plants are mustard garlic, honesty, and nasturtium. There are two generations a year. The pupa is the stage that hibernates. This is a migratory butterfly that sometimes flies in large swarms. It is a regular visitor of flower gardens.

mon butterfly in the Netherlands. Each year, there are three to five generations. Thus, the butterflies can be seen from mid-April to the beginning of October. The host plants are cabbage, radish, rape seed, nasturtium (Cruciferae) and species of reseda. The caterpillars grow extremely fast. They are usually full-grown within fourteen days and then they pupate. The Small White hibernates as a pupa. The colour of the pupa is green, brown or grey. This depends on the colour of the plant to which the pupa is fastened. A hibernating pupa would not be on a herbaceous plant, but on a tree trunk or stone. The Small White is a migratory butterfly that occasionally flies in swarms.

Pontia daplidice

Pontia daplidice, the Bath White, has an area of distribution ranging from the northern part of Africa and Europe to the eastern part of Asia. It is a fast flyer with nomadic tendencies. It is constantly searching for young reseda plants. The pupa is always fastened to a solid background, such as a tree trunk or a stone.

Pieris rapae, *the Small Cabbage White*

Pontia daplidice, *the Bath White*

Dryadula phaetusa

9 Heliconiidae – Heliconia

With a few exceptions, the butterflies belonging to the Heliconiidae or Heliconia family are only found in South and Central America.

The exceptions fly around the southern parts of the United States. The butterflies can be recognised immediately by their long, narrow wings and their long antennae. The wingspan varies from

Heliconius melpomene

about 6 to 10 centimetres. The wings are generally very colourful: bright red, yellow and black, sometimes alternating with blue.

They are very striking butterflies. Their bodies contain many substances that make them inedible for insectivores. The

Heliconius melpomene

vivid colours seem to give enemies the message: 'Just let me flutter by, I'm inedible anyway.' Their manner of flying is in keeping with this. They are simply very slow flyers that do not seem to be bothered by anything. They trust that their colours will be a sufficient warning to birds and other dangerous predators. A special characteristic of these butterflies is that they gather at common sleeping places at dusk. Large numbers of butterflies hang together in the trees to spend the night.

The first butterfly to rouse itself in the morning flies along the group of sleepyheads to wake them up. Heliconia owe their name 'passion flower butterflies' to

Heliconius charitonius

Sleeping place for Heliconius butterflies

the fact that the females lay their eggs almost exclusively on the leaves of the passiflora plant.

These plants contain toxic substances to prevent them from being devoured by herbivores.

The toxic substances, glycosides, contain cyanogenic groups that release cyanide, an extremely poisonous substance, during digestion.

The Heliconia caterpillars can eat the poisonous leaves and do not let themselves be frightened away. They are able to detoxify the substances by storing it in the fibres of their bodies. This sees to it that they are inedible.

The butterflies that develop from these caterpillars still have the toxic substances in their bodies, and are therefore inedible. They owe their toxicity to the

Heliconius *collects pollen*

mixes them with the pollen, which then becomes a liquid mix. The protein-rich liquid is then absorbed by the butterfly. The result is that some Heliconia can live for six months without hibernating.

A female of this butterfly species which is ready to mate sits and waits on a plant with her wings folded above her body. If a male suddenly flies over, she opens her wings.

If he sees a colour pattern that belongs to the females of his species, he will flutter in mid-air above her.

Once in a while he will dive down and brush his hind-wings against the female's antennae. On his hind wings he has scent scales which produce an

Heliconius melpomene *caterpillar*

passiflora plant. Heliconia get much older than the two or three weeks of most other butterfly species.

This is primarily due to the fact that they can absorb protein. Butterflies drink an enormous range of liquids: nectar, juice of rotting fruit, moisture from manure or dead animals, etc.

Water and the dissolved sugars contained in it are the main ingredients of these drinks.

If a Heliconia drinks nectar from a flower, pollen remains stuck to the tiny hairs on its proboscis. The butterfly exudes enzymes from its proboscis and

Display of Heliconius butterflies

aromatic substance, a so-called sex pheromone, which is typical of the species. This scent convinces the female that they are congeners. If this is actually the case, the dance ritual will end in mating. Heliconia males do not only

impregnate the female, but also transfer a number of proteins to her. So the female does not have to carry out the difficult task of forming the eggs all by herself.

The Heliconia females lay ten elongated, grooved eggs a day on the leaves and vines of the passiflora plant. The minute caterpillars that emerge from them eat and grow at a rapid pace.

Most of the caterpillars have spines that break off easily, thereby releasing the toxic substances. The pupate within three weeks.

Pupae of Heliconius melpomene

The spiny pupae hang on plant stems. They are beautifully camouflaged. They look more like a seed or a fruit than an insect. This way the pupae can get safely through the time it takes to undergo their metamorphosis.

The pupa stage does not usually last long. After about ten days, a colourful butterfly emerges.

Just pupated Heliconius melpomene

Agraulis vanillae

Agraulis vanillae (also called *Dione vanillae*) is a striking appearance among the Heleconiidae. It is found from the southern part of the United States and Florida to Peru in South America. It prefers to fly in open country where it visits the flowers of *Bidens pilosa* and lantana. They lay their eggs on species of passiflora which are avoided by most other members of the *Heliconius* family. The spiny caterpillars are inedible. This is also true of the beautiful butterflies, which are adorned on the underside of their wings with shining silver spots.

Dryas julia *caterpillar*

Dryadula phaetusa

Dryadula phaetusa is found from Mexico to Brazil. It has unusually short, wide wings for a member of the Heliconiidae family. Nor are the antennae very long. It

is a somewhat rare butterfly, which only lives in bushy areas. It does not live in forests. In contrast to other Heliconia, it does not gather pollen on its proboscis. It likes to drink nectar from asclepias flowers. The eggs are laid on *Passiflora talamancensis*.

Dryas julia *shows its orange top*

Dryas julia

The striking orange *Dryas julia*, which lives in South and Central America, deposits its eggs on the vines and leaves of different species of passiflora, such as *P. coeruleia*, *P. biflora*, *P. platyloba* and *P. vitifolia*. The caterpillars, which are beige with a pattern of brown spots, are well provided with spines. The pupa is rounded and provided with metallic spots. The butterfly rests with its wings folded against each other above its body. It then looks exactly like a withered leaf. Nothing can be seen of the bright orange colour and the butterfly is not bothered by troublesome insectivores. The butterflies are also difficult to catch, because they are very observant and can move fast and flexibly in the air.

The butterflies are often found on the flowers of *Lantana camara*, a flower very rich in nectar. It is anything but a rare butterfly. It flies all year round and in some periods it is present very large numbers.

Euides isabella

Euides isabella flies from Mexico to the Amazon region in South America. The butterflies are relatively small and have short antennae. Those of the males are generally black and those of the females yellow. The colour pattern closely resem-

Euides isabella

Heliconius charitonius

127

bles that of different *Heliconius* species; a nice case of mimicry. Euides can be recognised by the row of white spots along the edge of the wing. Butterflies of both sexes visit the flowers of low-growing herbs to the inflorescence in the tree-tops. The female deposits her eggs on *Passiflora platyloba* and *P. ambigua*, and sometimes on a neighbouring plant.

Heliconius charitonius

Heliconius charitonius has a large area of distribution. The butterfly is found in the Florida Everglades, in Central America and in the northern part of South America. The appearance of the butterfly is the same everywhere. There are no known subspecies or local variations of the 'zebra butterfly', despite its enormous area of distribution. The males of this species are very quick to start reproducing. They mate with the females while they are still emerging from the pupa. While the females are hanging to dry themselves after emerging, they are defenceless and cannot (yet) fly away. Moreover, the males are certain that they are mating with a virgin female. The females lay their eggs in groups on the young apical meristem of the different species of passiflora plants. The caterpillars of *H. charitonius* are even able to eat plants with barbs on their leaves and are therefore fatal for the caterpillars of other Heliconia butterflies.

Heliconius cydno

Heliconius cydno

Heliconius cydno

Heliconius cydno is found from Mexico to Colombia and Ecuador. The preferred host-plant is *Passiflora vitifolia* or *P. biflora*, but other passiflora plants are also used. The eggs are laid on the youngest vines of the plant. The butterflies like to fly in forests and the surrounding areas. Their favourite nectar

Heliconius cydno

plant is psiguria. The butterflies also gather large quantities of pollen from the flowers. Psiguria is therefore very important to both sexes, because they consider a place with a lot of flowers as their territory. Each day, they visit all the flowers and chase other Heliconia away. As in many other species of Heliconia, *Heliconius cydno* also appears in many different colour forms.

Heliconius erato

Heliconius erato

Heliconius erato appears in a particularly large number of subspecies and colour variations in an area ranging from Mexico to the Amazon region. The numerous forms are also similar to the many subspecies of *Heliconius melpomene*. Both species can best be distinguished by the form of the pupa. The pupa of H. erato has two horny protrusions, which that of *H. melpomene* lacks. Experts can distinguish the species on the basis of the difference in the scent exuded by the males when they display above the females. The host-plant of *H. erato* is *Passiflora talamancensis, P. coreacea* or *P. biflora*.

Heliconius hecale

Heliconius hecale is a relatively large Heliconia that is found from Mexico to Peru. It does not seem to have any preference for a certain type of territory, as it flies in open meadows and in tropical rainforests. The butterfly lays eggs on passiflora, but does not look for a certain species. *H. hecale* flies often and far. All these qualities make the butterfly one of the most common in Central and South America. Males and females visit many species of flowers, but are seen most often on psiguria. They do not tolerate any other Heliconia on 'their' flowers. It is a species with many forms, of which the butterfly in the photo looks a lot like *Euides isabella*, which is found in the same region.

Heliconius hortense

The area of distribution of Heliconius hortense ranges from Honduras to Ecuador. In contrast to most Heliconia, there are few colour variations. The differences are limited to the sizes of the yellow spots on the fore-wings.

Heliconius hecale

Heliconius hortense

H. hortense is especially striking because of its large wingspan, which can reach 7 centimetres. The host-plant is *Passiflora laurifolia*.

Heliconius melpomene

Heliconius melpomene flies from Mexico to Brazil. Dozens of subspecies are known. Each individual subspecies also has different forms, each of which looks like a subspecies of *H. erato*. Many studies have been devoted to this particularly complicated mimicry complex. *H. melpomene* prefers forest areas. It flies along the edges and in open spaces, but avoids the full sun. The butterflies gather pollen especially from psiguria flowers, but also

Heliconius melpomene

Heliconius melpomene

visit lantana and hamilia. Eggs are laid on the young leaves of passiflora plants. The caterpillars are white with black spots. Their head is orange-yellow. They also have a large number of spines on their body.

In captivity, this species can be bred very well, provided it is kept under the right circumstances.

It is a welcome guest in covered butterfly gardens, because it can be seen all year round as a butterfly that also likes to flutter around people.

Heliconius sara

Heliconius sara is one of the smallest Heliconia. Its area of distribution ranges from Mexico to the Amazon region. The females lay the eggs in groups of 20 to thirty on the apical meristems of their host-plants, the *Passiflora auriculata*. The caterpillars first eat the tender young leaves and when they are a bit larger the older leaves as well. The caterpillars

Heliconius sara

from one clutch of eggs slough almost simultaneously. The butterfly lives in tropical rainforests. The host-plant grows on the edge of those forests. Because the passiflora plant always grows in small areas, the appearance of *H. sara* is also very local. Nevertheless, it is not rare. The butterfly can become very old. The butterfly in the tropical butterfly garden of the Nooder Dierenpark in Emmen that lived the longest was a *H. sara* that flew about for almost seven months.

Thecla coronata, *top*

10 Lycaenidae – Hairstreaks, Coppers and Blues

More than 6,000 butterfly species belong to the family consisting of the Hairstreaks, Coppers and Blues. Nearly all of them are small butterflies. The largest has a wingspan of less than 8 centimetres.

Many species have a distinctive sheen on the upper side of the wing. Blues owe their name to the shiny metallic blue colour, often only found in the males. Coppers have striking red-coloured wings. Most of the time the different species can only be told apart by the pattern of markings on the underside of the wings. Many Hairstreaks have distinctive tails on their hind-wings. The extremely tiny eggs are covered with tiny pits and ridges. The small caterpillars which hatch out of these eggs, look more like snails.

Generally these caterpillars eat food rich in proteins: seeds, flower buds and sometimes insect larvae. A lot of Blue caterpillars, for example, live in an ants' nest for a long time. When the caterpillars are small, they let themselves be carried away by the worker ants of certain ant species, especially the myrmicinae, back to the nest. The ants find these caterpillars attractive because they secrete a

Thersamonia thersamon

sweet fluid for them. Once in the nest the caterpillars feed on ant larvae and on the food that the ants bring back to the nest. The pupa is also completed safely in the ants' nest. By making chirping sounds they keep the ants away. These Blues usually hatch out of the chrysalis early in the morning when the ants are not very active. This way they can leave the ants' nest in safety.

Most of the species are quite locally based. During their life-time the individual butterflies stay within an area with a radius of a few hundred metres.

Quercusia quercus, *the Purple Hairstreak*

Meleageria daphnis, *Meleager's Blue*

Hairstreaks

Callophrys rubi, *the Green Hairstreak*

The Callophrys rubi *caterpillar*

Callophrys rubi

Callophrys rubi, Green Hairstreak, can be found in an area extending from North Africa and Europe to as far as eastern Asia. It is a very small butterfly. The upper surfaces of the wings are brown and the undersides are shiny green. The caterpillars are not very fussy about their food and eat the growing points and flower buds of a wide range of plants belonging to the Cistaceae, Ericaceae, Leguminosae, Rhamnaceae and Rosaceae families. The butterflies drink the nectar of bird cherry and heather plants. The Green Hairstreak prefers the heather fields found on the edge of woods. There is one generation a year. They hybernate in the leaf litter as a pupa.

Eumaeus minyas

Eumaeus minyas

Eumaeus minyas is a relatively large and dark-coloured Blue, which flies in the warmer parts of the United States of America. The butterfly is likely to be found near shrubs growing on the edges of woods and in open areas in woods. The caterpillars live on plants which belong to the *Zamia* family (Zamiaceae). The dark-green sheen on the upper surface of the wings is not on the veins of the wings. The metallic blue markings on the outer margin of the hind-wings are striking.

Quercusia quercus, *the Purple Hairstreak*

Quercusia quercus

Quercusia quercus, Purple Hairstreak can be found in North Africa, Europe and Asia Minor. The butterflies catch the eye during flight because of the silver-grey colour of the underside of their wings. They are found flying around tree-

tops. Male Purple Hairstreaks form swarms around an isolated tree. The eggs are laid on oak trees. The eggs are laid between the buds of the oak tree, where they overwinter. When the time comes for the buds to open, the caterpillar has already hatched out. It starts to eat as soon as the buds burst open. This small Hairstreak only has one generation a year. The butterflies drink nectar and honeydew. They can be found in large numbers in suitable places near oak trees.

Satyrium acaciae

Satyrium acaciae, Sloe Hairstreak, can be found from Central Europe to Asia Minor. The wingspan of this very small Hairstreak is about 10 millimetres. Within its distribution area, it prefers areas with stony hillsides where small shrubs grow. The eggs are laid on the small blackthorn bushes. The female butterfly searches for suitable spots within the bushes to lay her eggs, five eggs at a time.

The eggs overwinter here. In the the spring, the butterfly's eggs hatch out at the same time as the buds on the blackthorn burst open. There is enough food for the caterpillars. There is one brood a year. The butterflies fly in July.

Satyrium ilicis, *the Ilex Hairstreak*

Satyrium ilicis

Satyrium ilicis, Ilex Hairstreak, can be found in both warm and cold areas from Western Europe to Asia Minor. The butterflies can be found in open spaces in woods or near edges of woods, wherever oak trees grow. The male Ilex Hairstreak like to drink nectar from the flowers on blackberry bushes. The females lay their eggs on the buds of oak trees (Fagaceae). They lay very few eggs, less than ten a day. The eggs overwinter. They hatch in the spring when the buds also start to open. The caterpillars grow quickly on the nutritious food. The chrysalis lies hidden under the leaf litter. The butterflies fly in July. There is one generation a year.

Satyrium spini, *the Blue-Spot Hairstreak*

Satyrium spini

Satyrium spini, Blue-spot Hairstreak can be found on stony hillsides and dry grasslands in Europe and western Asia. The butterflies drink nectar from the flowers of various herbs. They lay their eggs in groups of two to five in the axil of a branch of the buckthorn (Rhamnaceae), their host plant. The eggs stay there during the winter. The caterpillars hatch out just before the buds open. They grow quickly feeding on this nutritious leaf. There is, nevertheless, only one brood a year. The butterflies mainly fly in July.

Satyrium w-album

Satyrium w-album, White-letter Hairstreak, can be found in most parts of Europe and Asia as far as Japan. The

Satyrium w-album, *the White-Letter Hairstreak*

small brown butterfly with the characteristic white letter W on the underside of the wings drinks nectar and feeds on honeydew. The butterflies can mainly be found in woods where groups of elm trees grow close together. In suitable places like this, huge numbers of butterflies can be found flying around together. The females lay their eggs on the outer twigs of elm trees (Ulmaceae). The eggs overwinter there. In the spring, the caterpillars eat the buds and flowers of the elm tree. They eat the leaves at a later stage. The caterpillar pupates in cracks in the bark.

Thecla betulae, *the Brown Hairstreak*

Thecla betulae

Thecla betulae, Brown Hairstreak is found in the cool and temperate regions of Europe and Asia. They are quite small butterflies with a wingspan of less than 15 millimetres. The butterflies never fly long distances. Males and females look for the tallest tree on the edges of woods.

Here they drink honeydew. This tree is also used as a meeting spot. Females leave the treetops to lay their eggs on the low bushes of the blackthorn (Rosaceae). The females of this small Hairstreak do not usually lay more than about five eggs a day. The eggs overwinter on the blackthorn. As soon as the buds of the host plant open, the caterpillars hatch out. In June they pupate in the leaf litter. The butterflies are active in the summer. Brown Hairstreaks fly from the beginning of July until the end of September. An age of eight weeks is not unusual.

Thecla coronata, *underside*

Thecla coronata

Thecla coronata can be found in the tropical parts of South and Central America up to Mexico. Not only is it one of the largest but it is also one of the most beautiful representatives of the Lycaenidae family. The wingspan of the

males can reach up to 6 centimetres. The hind-wings of both sexes have long tails. The females distinguish themselves from the males by the striking red markings on the base of the tails. Another typical feature of this butterfly is the strongly indented edges of the hind-wings. The ventral surface of this Hairstreak has a beautiful green sheen with several dark stripes. Because the *Thecla coronata* rests with its wings held together in a vertical position above its body, it does not attract attention in between the leaves due to this pattern of colours.

Coppers

Lycaena alciphron, *the Purple-Shot Copper*

Lycaena alciphron

Lycaena alciphron, Purple-shot Copper, lives in dry grasslands from North Africa and Europe up to as far as Asia Minor. There is only one brood a year in the northern part of its distribution area and in the southern part sometimes two. The host plants of the caterpillar are sheep's sorrel and field sorrel (Polygoniaceae). The immature caterpillars hibernate in the leaf litter. The caterpillar grows in spring and at the beginning of summer. The butterfly flies in June, the purple sheen on its wings catches the eye.

Lycaena dispar, *the Large Copper*

Lycaena dispar batava

Lycaena dispar

Lycaena dispar, Large Copper, is in spite of its name quite a small butterfly. Its wingspan is about 20 millimetres. It is large compared to the other Coppers. It is found very locally in Europe and Asia. The subspecies *Lycaena dispar batava* can be found in the Netherlands in the

Lycaena dispar rutila

Overijsselse Weerribben. The bright orange-red coloured males defend a territory. The females are much less colourful and have a black pattern of markings on the upper side of the wings. The Large Copper lives in vast marshlands where it drinks nectar and searches for honeydew. The butterfly mainly lays its eggs on large aquatic sorrel plants and a few other sorrel species (Polygoniaceae). There is only one brood a year in the temperate regions, but in the more southerly regions there is sometimes up to three. The immature caterpillar hibernates in between the withered leaves at the base of large aquatic sorrel plants.

Lycaena hippothoe, *the Purple-Edged Copper*

Lycaena hippothoe

Lycaena hippothoe, Purple-edged Copper, lives in cold marshy areas in Europe and Asia. The male species can be recognised by the red colour with a blue sheen on the upper side of the wings. Females are predominantly brown. Because this butterfly only thrives in cool climates, there is only one generation a year. The butterflies fly in June and July. The host plant of the caterpillars is field sorrel (Polygoniaceae). The caterpillar hibernates when it is not completely fully grown. It grows very slowly. It goes into the chrysalis stage in the leaf litter.

Lycaena phlaeas

Lycaena phlaes, Small Copper, lives in both cold and very warm regions in

Lycaena phlaeas, *the Small Copper*

North Africa, Europe, Asia and North America. The butterfly is not really a migratory butterfly, but quickly colonises new territories where the host plants, field sorrel and sheep's sorrel (Polygoniaceae), grow. The butterflies fly from the beginning of May until the end of October with two to sometimes four broods. The immature caterpillar hibernates hidden between the leaves in the leaf litter. In the spring, the caterpillar soon grows and pupates into a loosely spun cocoon. Small Copper males are territorial. There is not much difference in appearance between the males and females.

Lycaena tityrus

Lycaena tityrus, Sooty Copper, lives in dry grasslands and heathlands in a region that reaches from Western Europe to Central Asia. In the warmer parts, there are sometimes as many as three generations a year. The host plants of the caterpillar are sheep's sorrel and field sorrel (Polygoniaceae). The immature caterpil-

Lycaena tityrus, *the Sooty Copper*

lars hibernate in between the withered leaves of the leaf litter. In the spring, the caterpillars grow quite quickly and pupate in May. The pupae hang, slightly hidden away, on the lowest parts of the host plant. There are two broods a year. The butterflies fly from May until September.

Lycaena virgaurae

Lycaena virgaurae, Scarce Copper, lives in the cool temperate regions of Europe and also in Asia as far as Mongolia. This

139

Lycaena virgaurae, *the Scarce Copper*

Blues

Agrodiaetus thersites, *Chapman's Blue*

butterfly distinguishes itself from the Large Copper by the white markings on the red ventral surface. The butterflies fly in July and August. There is only one brood a year. They search for nectar from flowers in grasslands, preferably on the edges of woods. The eggs are laid at the base of the stem of the host plant, the field sorrel (Polygoniaceae). The eggs overwinter there. The caterpillars which hatch out in the spring take more than 2 months to become adults. They pupate in June.

Agrodiaetus thersites

Agrodiaetus thersites, Chapman's Blue, lives in the warmer regions of North Africa, Europe and Asia. There are two to three generations a year. The host plant is sainfoin (Leguminosae). The small caterpillars hibernate in between the stones. In the spring, it takes a long time before the caterpillars become fully grown and they pupate in the leaf litter.

Lycaena virgaurae

Chapman's Blue survives even under difficult conditions. The butterflies drink nectar from flowers and water from between the stones on the riverbanks.

Aricia agestis, *underside*

Aricia agestis, *the Brown Argus, top*

Aricia agestis

Aricia agetis, Brown Argus, which lives in most parts of Europe and Asia, gets its name from the brown colour of both males and females.

The butterflies get easily mistaken for the brown-coloured females of other species of Blues.

Every year there are two to three broods. The half-grown caterpillar hibernates hidden in the leaf litter. The host plants are storksbill and sun rose (Cistaceae). In the spring, the caterpillar grows quickly and then pupates, also in the leaf litter. The butterflies can be seen from May until October.

Aricia artaxerxes, *the Scotch Argus*

Aricia artaxerxes

Aricia artaxerxes

Aricia artaxerxes, the Scotch Argus, can hardly be told apart from the Brown Argus. Most of the characteristics of these two species are the same. The Scotch Argus can survive extreme conditions and for this reason there is only one generation a year. The number of generations is the main difference between the two kinds of Argus.

Celastrina argiolus

Celastrina argiolus, the Holly Blue, lives in the region ranging from Central Europe to eastern parts of Asia. When in flight, the butterfly immediately catches the eye because of the silver-coloured underside of the wings. The butterfly lives in woods, parks and moorlands where the caterpillar's main host plants - alder tree, holly and ivy - are found. Holly Blue caterpillars can also live on

Celastrina argiolus, *the Holly Blue*

Danis danis, *underside*

many other plant species. The caterpillar feeds on buds and young leaves. It grows very rapidly on this nutritious food. Usually there is one, but sometimes a fourth generation. The pupa of the autumn brood hibernates on the host plant.

Danis danis, *top*

Cupido minimus, *the Little Blue*

Cupido minimas

Cupido minimas, Little Blue, is small, even for a Blue. The average wingspan is about 10 millimetres.

The small butterfly can be found dispersed over grasslands on calcareous soil in Europe and Asia. The Little Blue flies in June when the host plant of the caterpillar, the kidney vetch (Leguminosae) is in bloom. Eggs are laid on the flowers of the host plant. The caterpillar grows very quickly and hibernates at a fully grown stage on the withered flowers of the kidney vetch. It is a very vulnerable butterfly, because it is dependant on one type of host plant, which on top of that, has to be in bloom.

Danis danis

Danis danis, Danis Blue, has a distribution area which stretches from the Moluccas and Papua New Guinea to northeast Australia.

The caterpillars of this Blue eat the leaves of *Alphitonia excelsa* (Rhamnaceae).

This plant grows in open woodland. Both males and females like to rest on leaves at about two metres above the ground.

The noticeable white band on the upper side of the wings is characteristic for the genus *Danis.* This band is also on the underside of the wings of both males and females.

The white band is surrounded by a narrow band of a beautiful light green sheen. The wingspan of the *Danis danis* is between 3.5 and 4 centimetres.

Everes argiades, *the Short-Tailed Blue*

Everes argiades

Everes argiades, Short-tailed Blue, can be found in the warm and temperate regions of Europe and Asia. This very small butterfly, with a wingspan of just about 10 millimetres, can be recognised by the tails on the hind-wings. It flies in the vicinity of marshes and heaths. The host plant of this butterfly is bird's foot (Leguminosae). The caterpillars grow quickly. And so there are two to three broods a year. The fully grown caterpillar hibernates in the leaf litter.

Jamides alecto

Jamides alecto

Jamides alecto is a Southeast Asian Blue which is quite common in an area stretching from Sri Lanka and India to Burma and Malaysia. It likes to fly in hilly or mountainous areas with woodlands in which the host plant *Elettaria cardamomum* can be found. The butter-

flies fly quite near the ground and are certainly not strong flyers. The caterpillars feed on the flowers and fruits of the host plant. Because this plant is used in Eastern medicine and for cooking Asian food, the caterpillars are seen as pests. The females have a dark pattern of markings along the edge of the hind-wings, while the blue colour on the males is much lighter and brighter. The wingspan of *Jamides alecto* is about 3.5 to 4.5 centimetres. The hind-wings are decorated by tails.

Lycaeides argyrognomon, *Reverdin's Blue*

Lycaeides argyrognomon

Lycaedes argyrognomon, Reverdin's Blue, lives in the warmer regions of Europe and Asia. This Blue has two generations a year. Its host plant is crown vetch (Leguminosae). The second brood of females lay their eggs on the woody parts of the host plant. The eggs overwinter there. The females lay their eggs on the leaves of the crown vetch at the beginning of summer. Within a week, the caterpillars hatch out and grow very quickly and pupate. The butterflies fly in June and August.

Lysandra bellargus

Lysandra bellargus, Ardonis Blue, is bright blue-coloured butterfly, which lives in a large part of Europe to far into Asia. There are two generations a year. The butterflies mainly fly in June and September.

Lysandra bellargus, *the Adonis Blue*

Lysandra coridon

They lay their eggs on horseshoe vetch and crown vetch (Leguminosae). Shortly after the caterpillar hatches out of the egg it hibernates on the host plant.

Maculinea alcon, *the Alcon Blue*

Lysandra coridon, *the Chalkhill Blue*

Lysandra coridon

Lysandra coridon, Chalk-hill Blue, can be found scattered over a large part of Europe. There is one brood every year, the males are pale blue in colour and the females are brown. The host plant of the caterpillar of this Blue is horseshoe vetch (Leguminosae). The eggs are laid on the strong woody parts of the plant, where they will overwinter. The caterpillars grow very slowly in the spring. Sometimes it takes up to four months for them to pupate. The butterfly which emerges from the chrysalis not only feeds on the nectar of flowers but also drinks the moisture in manure.

Maculinea alcon

Maculinea alcon, Alcon Blue, lives in a region that stretches from Western Europe to Central Asia. It lives in wet moorlands, where heather and bog gentian grow. These Blues needs to find myrmicinae to look after their caterpillars. After mating, the females search for bog gentian plants to lay their eggs on.

Maculinea alcon

of these plants. Then the immature caterpillars get carried away by myrmicinea to the ants' nest under the ground. The caterpillars hibernate here. In the spring, the caterpillars eat a large number of ant larvae. The caterpillar of the Large Blue also pupates in the ants' nest. The butterfly emerges from the pupa and leaves the host's nest. There is one brood a year. The butterflies fly in July and August.

They prefer to lay them in the flower. As soon as the caterpillars have hatched out, they eat their way to the ovary where they eat the ovules. The immature caterpillars leave the flowers and let themselves be carried off by ants to the underground ants' nest. Here they hibernate. In the spring, the caterpillars feed on ant larvae until they pupate, this also takes place in the ants' nest. In July and August, the butterflies fly out of the ants' nest. There is one generation of Alcon Blues a year.

Maculinea telejus, *the Scarce Large Blue*

Maculinea arion, *the Large Blue*

Maculinea arion

Maculinea arion, Large Blue, can be found throughout Europe and Asia. In rocky areas where few plants grow, the butterfly searches for the nectar of flowering thyme plants. Eggs are laid on thyme and wild marjoram (Labiatae). The caterpillars eat the nutritious ovaries

Maculinea telejus

Maculinea telejus, Scarce Large Blue, can be found in the warm and temperate regions of Europe and Asia. The butterflies search for nectar in the flowers of the greater burnet saxifrage (Rosaceae). The eggs are also laid in these flowers. In the late summer, the caterpillars of the Scarce Large Blue eat the ovaries of the plant. The immature caterpillar leaves the host plant to be taken away by the myrmicine worker ants. Once in the ants' nest, the caterpillar eats lots of ant larvae. The caterpillar also hibernates here. In the spring, it carries on eating the ant larvae until it pupates in June. These butterflies, which do not live much longer than a week, fly in the summer. There is one brood of Scarce Large Blues a year.

Plebejus argus, *the Silver-Studded Blue*

Meleageria daphnis

Meleageria daphnis, *Meleager's Blue*

Meleageria daphnis

Meleageria daphnis, Meleager's Blue, lives in the warm and quite dry regions of southeast Europe. The butterfly prefers stony hillsides sparsely covered with vegetation. The host plant is crown vetch (Leguminosae). The eggs overwinter on this plant. The caterpillar, which hatches out in the spring, keeps feeding and growing until it pupates at the end of May. These butterflies, whose hindwings are strongly serrated, fly in July and August.

Plebejus argus

Plebejus argus, Silver-studded Blue, can be found on heathlands in Europe and Asia, as far as Japan. The colour of the upper surface of the wings is blue in the males and brown in the females. The host plants of the caterpillar are ling and heather (Ericaceae). The eggs are laid on the woody stems, where they hibernate. In the spring, the caterpillars feed on the flower buds and growing points, preferably of young heather plants. The young caterpillars let themselves be taken by

146

Plebejus argus

Plebicula dorylas, *the Turquoise Blue*

Blue hibernates on the host plant. In spring, it feeds on flower buds and young leaves. The pupa lies hidden in the leaf litter. There is one generation a year, and the butterflies fly in July.

Polyommatus Icarus, *the Common Blue*

worker ants to the ants' nest, where they pupate. Some of the Silver-studded Blues can also survive outside an ants' nest. The butterflies live together in large numbers in quite small areas.

Polyommatus icarus

Polyommatus icarus, Common Blue, is common in a large range of climates in North Africa, Europe, as far as eastern

Plebicula dorylas, *the Turquoise Blue*

Plebicula dorylas

Plebicula dorylas, Turquoise Blue, can be found very locally in Europe and Asia Minor. The males of these small butterflies are noticeable because of their unique light blue colour. This colour gives these butterflies their name. This Blue's host plant is kidney vetch (Leguminosae). Females only lay their eggs on young plants which are not in bloom. While it is still small, the caterpillar lives and grows inside the thick, fleshy leaves. The small caterpillar of the Turquoise

Polyommatus icarus

Asia. It can be found in all kinds of grasslands and heathlands where the host plant grows. The main host plant of this caterpillar is bird's foot (Leguminosae). The Common Blue hibernates as an immature caterpillar. In the spring, the caterpillar grows very slowly. It takes more than two months before it pupates. The chrysalis lies hidden in the leaf litter. There is one brood a year. In the warmer parts of the distribution area there may even be two to three broods a year.

Pseudophilotes baton, *the Baton Blue*

Polyommatus icarus

Pseudophilotes baton

Pseudophilotes baton, Baton Blue, lives in dry grasslands and steppes in Europe and Central Asia. There are two broods a year. The caterpillars live on flowers and fruits of different types of thyme plants (Labiatae). The immature caterpillars of the autumn brood hibernate in the leaf litter. The following spring they grow quickly until they pupate. The caterpillars of the second brood also grow quickly.

Scolitantides orion

Scolitantides orion, Chequered Blue, has a distribution area covering the rocky hillsides of Europe and Asia. The host plants of the caterpillar are succulents (Crassulaceae) such as stonecrop and sedum. They eat a lot of these plants very quickly and are fully grown within a month. They hibernate as a pupa fastened to the bottom of a stone by a thread. In the warmer regions of its distribution area, the Chequered Blue has a second

Scolitantides orion, *the Chequered Blue*

brood. The butterflies from the summer brood are a much darker colour than the spring brood.

Talicada nyseus

Talicada nyseus

Talicada nyseus is a Blue that lives in the southern parts of India and in Sri Lanka. There is no difference in appearance between the males and females of this species. The butterflies alternate between flying short distances and then resting for a while on the ground. They are active until twilight. They usually fly near to the ground in jungles and drier regions. The eggs are laid on the leaves of succulents (Crassulaceae). The caterpillars make tunnels in the leaves and live there hidden away from insect eaters. The pupation does not usually take any longer than a week.

Vacciniina optilete, *the Cranberry Blue*

Vacciniina optilete

Vacciniia optilete, Cranberry Blue, lives in a small locality in the cool temperate regions in Europe, Asia and North America. They can only be found near fens, in which peat moors develop, and which are scattered through the woods. Only here can the caterpillar find its host plant, the cranberry. The caterpillars hibernate deeply hidden away in the peat. In May they eat young shoots and the ovaries of cranberry plants. When they are fully grown, they crawl out of the peat to pupate. The Cranberry Blue's main source of nectar is heather. There is just one generation a year. The flight time is in July.

Maniola jurtina, *the Meadow Brown*

11 Satyridae – Browns

Mycalesis remulina

Coenonympha pamphilus, *the Small Heath lays eggs*

Brintesia circe, *the Great Banded Grayling*

The butterflies which belong to the family Satyridae or Browns are usually inconspicuous and brown coloured. They have circular eye-spots on the undersides of their wings, which is where they get their family name from. This description matches almost all of the 3,000 members of the Browns. More lavishly coloured Browns can only be found in tropical parts of South America. It is not always easy to correctly identify the species of butterfly from this family. This, for example, applies to the butterflies belonging to the genus *Erebia*. A very large number of similar looking species of this genus can be found in the mountainous areas in Europe and Asia.

Many of these butterflies can be found on rotting fruit and seem to take in the moulds along with the juice. Honeydew is also a very important source of food. Nectar is not very important as a source of food for many of these butterflies. Most of the species fly near to the ground and like to rest in sunny places. The host plant is nearly always a plant belonging to the grass family. Some of the females do not even really lay their eggs on the plants, since while flying over a tussock of grass they just let the eggs drop. Caterpillars with forked tails hatch out of these spherical eggs which have longitudinal grooves. These caterpillars, which are not very brightly coloured, are either smooth or have lots of rounded outgrowths.

The caterpillars grow very slowly, a growing period of 4 to 6 months is no

Lasiommata megera, *the Wall Butterfly*

Lethe samio

summer here without the risk of drying out. This is an extremely unusual place for a chrysalis of a butterfly to be.

Aphantopus hyperantus

The Ringlet, *Aphantopus hyperantus*, is common in Europe and Asia.

The preferred habitat of this butterfly is meadows and other grasslands in the vicinity of woods. The butterfly is the prototype of a Brown, namely a brown butterfly with rather small eye-spots, which sometimes are no more than dots. It only has one generation a year. The caterpillars grow particularly slowly. Ages of 10 to 11 months are no exception. Hibernation is in the form of an immature caterpillar.

The caterpillars eat plants belonging to the grass and sedge families. The butterfly can be found in large numbers in areas where it has the right habitat.

exception. This is due to the fact that the grasses they eat are difficult to digest. For some species, the whole development process from egg to butterfly can take up to two years. The grasses and bamboos that the caterpillars eat do not contain poisonous substances. Because of this, these caterpillars and butterflies are very edible to birds and other insect eaters.

The pupae of some of the European species, like the Grayling, find a safe place under the ground. They spend the

Aphantopus hyperantus, *the Ringlet*

Brintesia circe, *Great Banded Grayling*

Brintesia circe

Brintesia circe, the Great Banded Grayling, lives in the hot to very hot regions stretching from Europe to Central Asia. This large butterfly with a noticeable white band across the wings can be found in grassy areas on the edge of woods. The host plants are different types of grasses (Graminae). Immediately after hatching out the caterpillar looks for a suitable stalk of grass to hibernate on. It is not until the following spring and early summer that they start to feed and grow. The pupa of the Great Banded Grayling lies hidden away in a hole under the ground. There is one brood a year. The butterflies fly in August.

Coenonympha arcania, *Pearly Heath*

Coenonympha arcania

Coenonympha arcania, Pearly Heath, lives all over Europe and the western part of Asia. When these butterflies fly, the orange fore-wings and the dark grey hind-wings catch the eye. The butterfly lives on nectar from the flowers of bushes which grow on quite dry ground. The eggs are laid on several types of grass (Graminae) and sedge (Cyperaceae). The Pearly Heath caterpillar grows slowly. It pupates at the end of May or the beginning of June. The chrysalis hangs in between the vegetation. There is one generation a year. The butterflies swarm locally in large numbers at the end of June and the beginning of July.

Coenonympha glycerion, *Chestnut Heath*

Coenonympha glycerion

Coenonympha glycerion, Chestnut Heath, lives in the temperate regions of Europe and Asia. Its preferred habitat is grassland near marshes. The butterfly lays its eggs on grasses (Graminae). The immature caterpillar hibernates in the vegetation. It takes quite a while before the caterpillar starts to feed and grow in the spring. The pupa hangs from the stalk of a plant. There is one brood of Chestnut Heaths a year. This butterfly can be found in large numbers in a small local area.

Coenonympha pamphilus

The Small Heath, *Coenonympha pamphilus*, is one of the smallest Browns. The average wingspan is about 3 centimetres. The butterfly has a distribution area which stretches from North Africa through Europe to Asia. It can live in

Coenonympha pamphilus, *Small Heath*

Erebia medusa, *Woodland Ringlet*

grasslands under a wide variety of conditions. The caterpillars live on various grass species. Since some of the plants are more nutritious than others there is quite a difference in the growth rates of the caterpillars. As a result
the butterflies can be found for a long period of the year, even though there is usually only one brood a year. The immature caterpillar prefers to hibernate in grasses which stay green in winter. This means that it can also feed on warm winter days. It is quite a common butterfly.

Erebia medusa

Erebia medusa, Woodland Ringlet, lives in temperate regions from Europe to Central Asia. Dozens of species of the genus *Erebia* are known. The butterflies differ in the pattern of markings on the wings. The Woodland Ringlet likes wet grasslands. Not only can it find nectar here but also the caterpillar's host plants: grasses (Graminae) and sedges (Cyperaceae). The caterpillars grow slowly. They hibernate at the immature stage in

Hipparchia fagi, *Woodland Grayling*

a dried-up tussock of grass. The pupa lies between the withered leaves in the leaf litter. The butterflies fly in June.

Hipparchia fagi

Hipparchia fagi, Woodland Grayling, has its habitat in woods in a large part of Europe. The butterflies prefer to stay near the edges of woods. They drink nectar from flowers and the juices of rotting fruit and sap oozing from trees. Eggs are laid on a large variety of grass species (Graminae). The immature caterpillar hibernates on a dry grass stalk. After the hibernation, it feeds for quite some time before it pupates in a hole under the ground. There is one generation a year. Woodland Graylings mainly fly in August.

Hipparchia semele, *Grayling*

Hipparchia semele

The Grayling, *Hipparchia semele*, lives in the lower lying areas of Europe and the western part of Asia. Due to the colours and markings on the underside of the wings, the butterfly is hardly noticeable when it holds its wings up against each other. When resting it likes to sit on the bare ground in the sun or on a tree trunk. The butterfly feeds on the sap oozing from trees and on nectar. The caterpillar's host plants are various species of grass, such as grey hair grass (Corynephorus) and sheep's fescue. The caterpillar feeds and grows in autumn and the next spring. This caterpillar also hibernates, hidden away deep in a

tussock of grass. In June, it is fully grown and pupates underneath the ground. It stays here for about six weeks so as not to risk drying out. When the female butterflies emerge from the pupa, the eggs have not yet developed in their bodies. They have to drink nectar for at least two weeks before they are able to lay eggs. Especially in the hotter regions, female Graylings can reach an age of 3 months.

Lasiommata megera, *Wall Brown*

Lasiommata megera

The Wall Brown, *Lasiommata megera*, has a large distribution area that stretches from North Africa, southern and Central Europe up to Asia. It lives in grasslands in many regions and can usually be found on stones and rocks. The colour on the underside of the wings is adapted to this habitat and so the butterfly is hard to see when resting. The upper side of the wings is much more colourful, with a dark band on the male's fore-wings. There are two to three broods a year. The caterpillars live on a wide variety of grass species. The Wall Browns hibernates as an immature caterpillar. The butterflies drink nectar from the flowers of herbs and bushes.

Lasiommata maera

Lasiommata maera, Large Wall Brown, can be found in North Africa and Europe to as far as Central Asia. The butterfly looks very similar to *Lasiommata megera*, but is a bit larger. Another

Lasiommata maera, *Large Wall Brown*

Lethe europa, *dorsal surface*

important difference are the two white spots in the large eye-spot on the top of the underside of the fore-wing. This butterfly usually flies around stony areas and near rocky slopes. The caterpillars of the Large Wall Brown feed on grasses (Graminae). The immature caterpillar hibernates in a withered tussock of grass. There is one and sometimes a second generation of this butterfly a year.

Lethe europa

Lethe europa lives in the region stretching from India and Pakistan to China and Taiwan in northern Asia and as far as the Philippines and Indonesia in the south. It is a species which belongs to an extensive genus of large, brown-coloured butterflies, which mainly live in Asia, but a few species can also be found in America. The host plant of the caterpillars is bamboo (Graminae). This butterfly is mainly active in the early morning and in the

Lethe europa, *ventral surface*

evening. In the rainy season in Southeast Asia it flies in large numbers. *Lethe europa* has a wingspan of 6.5 to 7.5 centimetres and its dorsal surface is a dark-brown colour. On the underside of the hind-wing, the butterfly has several large eye-spots. The female has a wide white diagonal stripe over the fore-wings.

Maniola jurtina

The Meadow Brown, *Maniola jurtina*, can be found in a large part of Europe and in those parts of Africa and Asia which border onto Europe. It has a powerful flight and searches for its food in flowering meadows, banks and wooded banks. There is only one generation a year, which can be spotted from June up to September. The reason for this is that not all of the butterflies come out of the pupal stage at the same time. Males defend their own territory against their own kind. Females spend a lot of time searching for nectar. They need a lot of nutritious food to produce eggs. The eggs are laid on a large variety of grasses. The caterpillars are not very selective. The immature caterpillar hibernates in a withered tussock of grass. They carry on feeding unless the winter is too cold.

Melanargia galathea

The Marbled White, *Melanargia galathea*, can be recognised immediately by the striking black and white markings on

Maniola jurtina

Melanargia galathea, *Marbled White*

Melanargia galathea

the upper side of the wings. The butterfly is widespread in Central Europe, but can also be found in North Africa and in the western parts of Asia. The patterns of colour on the underside of the wings of the males and females are different. The butterflies are quite slow flyers and forage a lot on thistles. The female only lays a few eggs a day, usually less than ten. The butterflies live for more than a month and they are carrying eggs when they come out of the chrysalis. The caterpillars, which live on grasses, grow very

slowly. The caterpillar hibernates soon after it hatches out of the egg, even before it has eaten anything. When the caterpillar is fully grown it pupates in the leaf litter.

Melanitis leda

Melanitis leda is a typical representative of the genus *Melanitis*, which can be found in the woodlands of Africa, Asia and Australia. The butterflies are only active at sunrise and sunset. The male

157

Melanitis leda, *ventral surface*

Melanitis leda *from Tanzania*

Melanitis leda, *dorsal surface*

occupies a kind of territory and immediately flies towards anything that moves. It even approaches large animals and people to investigate them. It rests in between dead leaves during the day and because of its colour it can not be seen there. When disturbed it flies off a little way further on and settles down again in between the dead leaves. The butterflies drink the juices of rotting fruit and the sap oozing out of damaged trees. The female lays her eggs on grasses. Because they lay them on rice and sugarcane

Minois dryas, *Dryad*

(Sacharum) in Southeast Asia, the butterfly can cause damage to plantations. In Africa, the caterpillar lives on *Cynodon setaria*, in Australia on *Imperata cylindrica*, *Imperata conferta* and various other species of *Sacharum* (Poaceae). The generations of *Melanitis leda* which hatch out at different times of the year are clearly distinguishable. In Australia, the eye-spots on the wings of the summer brood are clearly visible but are either non-existent or very vague in the winter brood. In Africa, the brood from the dry season does not have these eye-spots and so it looks more like a dead leaf. The wingspan is between 6 and 8.5 centimetres. The markings and colour of the males and females are almost identical.

Minois dryas

Minois dryas, Dryad, has a distribution area which stretches over the hotter parts of Europe and Asia, to as far as Japan. The butterfly can be found in grasslands near marshy areas. The caterpillars live on grasses (Graminae). They grow very slowly and hibernate as a tiny caterpillar in the vegetation. In the spring and early summer, the Dryad caterpillars also grow slowly. The pupa lies hidden beneath the ground in a hole. There is one generation a year. The butterflies fly mainly in August.

Mycalesis rhacotis

Mycalesis rhacotis is very common in the part of Africa south of the Sahara. The butterfly is active throughout the year and many can be found in shady places in forests. It mainly shows itself in the morning and towards evening time. It is a weak flyer, flying near the ground and resting frequently on the grass. The wingspan of this predominantly brown butterfly varies between 4 and 5 centimetres. Its appearance differs in each season, especially in the size and colour of the larger eye-spots on the wings. The caterpillars of this butterfly species feed on *Ehrharta erecta* grass species (Graminae).

Mycalesis terminus

Mycalesis terminus lives in Australia, on New Guinea and on many other islands belonging to the Bismarck Archipelago and the Moluccas. It can be found in large numbers and can be seen as a butterfly throughout the year. In Australia, the chrysalis stage, which normally takes at least three weeks, is restricted to twelve days in April and May. The appearance of the butterfly changes with the seasons. In the dry season, from September to November, the brown colour is much lighter and the eye-spots are less clear. Transitional forms of the butterflies from the wet and dry seasons can sometimes be found. The males and females of this butterfly are almost identical and have a wingspan of about 4 centimetres. The caterpillars live on grasses such as *Imperata* (Graminae).

Neorina krishna

The distribution area of *Neorina krishna* is restricted to Java. It is one of the largest butterflies of the family Satyridae. It can reach a wingspan of more than 9 centimetres. The basic colour is dark-brown. A light yellow to orange-coloured band runs diagonally across the fore-wings. Between this band and the edge of the fore-wing is a large dark eye-spot. There are two smaller eye-spots on the outer margin of the hind-wing. The butterfly also has tails on the hind-wings.

Pararge aegeria

Pararge aegeria, Speckled Wood, is a

Neorina krishna

Pyronia tithonus, *Gatekeeper*

butterfly which is found in the deciduous forests of North Africa, Europe and Central Asia. Because it likes to live in woods where oak and birch trees grow, it can rarely be found above a height of 1,000 metres. When a butterfly, it is active from spring until autumn and has two broods. During this period, the slower growing butterflies from the first brood fly together with the fastest ones from the second brood. The butterflies feed on nectar and on sap oozing out of trees, but can also be found on excrement. The caterpillar's host plants are grasses. Some of the caterpillars grow quickly and pupate within a month, others do not do this until after six months. The chrysalis stage of the first generation takes two weeks. The Speckled Wood hibernates as a pupa and in some parts of its distribution area also as a caterpillar.

Pyronia tithonus

Pyronia tithonus, Gatekeeper, is an inhabitant of temperate and warm regions in Europe and the western part of Asia.

Pararge aegeria, *Speckled Wood*

The butterfly can be recognised by the two white dots in the black eye-spots on the underside of the fore-wing. It can usually be found on grasslands on the edges of woods. The Gatekeeper gets a lot of nectar from flowering blackberry bushes. The butterfly lays its eggs on grasses (Graminae). The caterpillars grow slowly. The immature caterpillar hibernates on a dry grass stalk. The second growing period is in the spring and early summer and continues until pupation. The pupa lies in the leaf litter. There is one generation a year. They fly in July and August.

Araschnia levana

12 Nymphalidae – Tortoiseshells, Fritillaries and Purple Emperors

The Nymphalidae family is one of the largest butterfly families. It includes many thousands of butterfly species throughout the world. They vary in size from butterflies with a wingspan of 25 millimetres to butterflies with a wingspan as large as 150 millimetres. Butterflies in this family have a distinctive way of flying. After every wingbeat, they hold their wings stretched out from their body and glide for a while without moving their wings. When on the ground, the butterflies can often be found near dead animals, fruit fallen from a tree or the rotting parts of plants. They suck all manner of juices from these rotting things, which they need to make their pheromones for example. When a butterfly in this family settles down to rest on a plant, it usually holds its head bent down and its wings held up together above its body. These butterflies hold on to objects with two pairs of legs. The front pair of legs is inconspicuous and most of the time they are not even visible. But this gives the wrong impression. It is only that the two front legs are much smaller than the other four. They

Clossiana dia, *Weaver's Fritillary*

are not used for walking or for holding on to things, but for cleaning their antennae and other parts of their body. The eggs are round to oval in shape and usually have grooves and ridges. Sometimes the eggs are laid together in large batches on the host plant.

The Map Butterfly lays its eggs in clusters of six to ten. Most of the caterpillars of the butterflies belonging to this family have large spines and some also have lots of small spines. The pupae hang on stalks or under leaves and are well disguised as fruit, seeds or other parts of a plant.

Precis tugela

Aglais urticae, *Small Tortoiseshell*

Tortoiseshell Butterflies

Aglais urticae

Araschnia levana, *Map Butterfly*

Araschnia levana

Aglais urticae

Aglais urticae, Small Tortoiseshell, has a distribution area stretching from Europe to eastern Asia. The butterflies drink nectar from the flowers of herbaceous plants and bushes. The females search for the young plants of the large stinging nettle (Urticaceae) on which to lay large numbers of eggs. There are between one and three generations a year. The Small Tortoiseshell hibernates as a butterfly, usually in lofts or in sheds and stables. In the Netherlands, it is one of the most common butterflies.

The caterpillar of Araschnia levana

Araschnia levana

Araschnia levana, Map Butterfly, is a small butterfly with colourful markings, which can be found in a large part of Europe and Asia. There are two easily distinguishable broods. The spring brood is orange and has a pattern of dark markings and those of the summer brood are dark coloured with a white band. The butterflies drink nectar from the flowers of herbaceous plants and from bushes such as the blackberry. Female Map Butterflies lay their eggs in clusters on the underside of the leaf of their host plant, the large stinging nettle (Urticaceae). This species of butterfly hibernates as a pupa.

Cethosia biblis

Cethosia biblis can be found in India, Pakistan, China, Burma, Malaysia, Indonesia and the Philippines. The caterpillars, which have poisonous spines, live together in groups of five to six on plants belonging to the genus Passiflora. The butterflies are also poisonous. They give a warning about this by the striking red colour of the upper sides of the wings. When resting, they hold their wings fold-

Cethosia biblis

ed together vertically above their body. The pattern on the underside, which can be seen then, looks like written lines in a book. This is the butterfly's namesake (biblis means book).

Cethosia hypsea

Cethosia hypsea

Cethosia hypsea

Cethosia hypsea can be found in Burma, Malaysia and Indonesia. The caterpillars live on *Adenia* and other poisonous passifloraceous plants. Not only are the striped caterpillars poisonous, but they also have spines, even on their heads. The butterflies are also poisonous and the striking red colour on the upper side of the wings is a warning against this. *Cethosia hypsea* visits many flowers.

Cynthia cardui, *Painted Lady*

Cynthia cardui

Cynthia cardui, Painted Lady, can be found throughout most of the world except for South America. In Europe, it is one of the most well-known migratory butterflies. During the winter, the butterfly lives in the northern part of Africa. In the spring, it migrates northwards to Europe, sometimes as far north as Finland. The butterflies mate and lay their eggs on thistles (Compositae), stinging nettles (Urticaceae) and various other plant species. The caterpillars grow quickly, pupate and before autumn a new brood of butterflies is flying around. Most of them stay in the vicinity of their birthplace, but they cannot hibernate in the northern parts of Europe and so they die. But some manage to fly back to the area around the Mediterranean. This is where the Painted Ladies do hibernate. In the following spring, their descendants take up the same trek, flying thou-

Cynthia cardui *from Australia*

sands of kilometres to Europe. The Australian species has small blue marks on the hind-wings.

Inachis io

Inachis io, the Peacock Butterfly, lives in Europe and the northern part of Asia. The butterfly hibernates in cool, rather wet areas. In the Netherlands, it is one of the first butterflies to be seen in the spring. The female Peacocks lay their eggs in large numbers on large clumps of stinging

IInachis io, *Peacock*

Caterpillars of Inachis io

Eggs of Inachis io

nettles (Urticaceae), which grow on the edges of woods or on the banks of streams. The caterpillars live together in large numbers and together they eat stinging nettles, one after the other. When the time comes to pupate, each caterpillar searches individually for a suitable and safe place. The golden coloured pupae are hardly noticeable. The eyes on the upper side of the hind-wings play a large part in the self-defence mechanism of this butterfly. A hungry predator such as a bird can be frightened off by these eyes. If not, the bird will try to peck the butterfly in the (fake) eyes. The wings get a bit damaged by this, but the butterfly is alarmed and flies away immediately.

Nymphalis antiopa, *Camberwell Beaty*

Nymphalis antiopa

Nymphalis antiopa, Camberwell Beauty, can be found in Europe, Asia and North America. This large butterfly lives in woods, where it searches for sap seeping from trees and juices of rotting fruit. The butterfly lays eggs, hundreds at a time, on birch trees (Betulaceae) and willows (Salicaceae). The caterpillars live together in large numbers on the host plants. The caterpillars grow at the beginning of the summer. There is one brood of butterflies a year, which emerge from the chrysalis before winter. Camberwell Beauties hibernate as butterflies hidden away in hollow trees or other sheltered places.

Nymphalis polychloros, *Large Tortoiseshell*

Nymphalis polychloros

Nymphalis polychloros, Large Tortoiseshell, can be found in the northern parts of Africa, Europe and Central Asia. These large butterflies live on the edges of forests, where they search for sap oozing out of trees and juices of rotting fruit. The female lays the eggs in groups of 100 to 200 on the twigs of elms (Ulmaceae) and willows (Salicaceae). Isolated trees are especially attractive to lay their eggs on. There is one generation a year. The Large Tortoiseshell hibernates as a butterfly in a hollow tree or in some other sheltered place.

Pantoporia perius

Pantoporia perius can be found in the Himalayas, India, Burma, Malaysia and the southern part of China. The butterflies have a distinctive way of flying. After several fast wingbeats, they glide for a while with their wings stretched out

Pantoporia perius

Polygonia c-album

Pantoporia perius *with open wings*

eastern part of Asia. The butterflies can be found in many different types of climate. Not only do they feed on nectar but also on the juices of rotting fruit. The butterfly flies long distances searching for suitable host plants. Stinging nettles (Urticaceae), hop (Cannabaceae) and elm (Ulmaceae) are the particular favourites. The butterfly hibernates in the adult stage, disguised as a dry leaf in the leaf litter.

Precis almana

horizontally. The black and white markings on the upper sides of the wings makes the butterfly inconspicuous in both the sunny and shady parts of the forest.

Polygonia c-album, *Comma Butterfly*

Polygonia c-album

Polygonia c-album, the Comma Butterfly, has a distribution area stretching from North Africa through Europe to the

Precis (Junonia) almana

*Precis almana*is is a representative of a butterfly genus which lives in all the tropical regions of the world. Butterflies of the *Precis* species usually have bright colours and striking eye-spots on their wings. When looking for flowers, the butterflies fly very fast keeping close to the ground. The caterpillars live on various plants such as plantain (Plantaginaceae) and bear's breeches (Acan-

Precis atlites

plant of *Precis atlites* is *Hygrophila*. When the butterfly walks across a flower searching for nectar, it keeps closing its wings and suddenly opening them again. Some of the other butterflies of the Nymphalidae family also have this same way of walking across flowers.

Precis (Junonia) hedonia

Precis hedonia can be found in Malaysia, New Guinea and Australia. The butterfly has a preference for marshy

thaceae). The males and females have the same pattern of colour. The colours in the wet season can differ quite a lot from those in the dry season.

Precis hedonia

Precis atlites

Precis atlites is a butterfly which can be found in southwest Asia from India to the southern part of China. The butterfly has a characteristic way of flying, in which short gliding flights alternate with sitting on the ground for a short time. The host

Precis hedonia

areas surrounded by forests. The caterpillar's host plants are *Hygrofila salicifolia* and *Hemigraphis alternata* (Acanthaceae). The pattern of colour on these butterflies is not consistent, but varies from season to season. They are slow flyers and they keep landing on grasses or tree trunks for a while. The butterflies usually rest on trees one to two metres above the ground with their head bent downwards. They then hold their wings together above their bodies and because of their shape and colour they look exactly like dead leaves. They spend the night in this position in large groups altogether.

Precis iphita

Precis (Junonia) iphita

Precis iphita lives in Sri Lanka, India, Pakistan and Burma. It is a dark-coloured butterfly and even the eye-spots on the wings are much smaller than on most of the other *Precis* species. In the wet forest areas of its distribution area, it is a common butterfly species. *Precis iphita* mainly rests in the shade, but in very wet areas it also rests in the sun. It can be found up to a height of nearly 3,000 metres. In Sri Lanka, where it is a migratory butterfly, it frequently flies long distances with many other butterflies of the same sort. The males and females of this butterfly, which has a wingspan of between 5.5 and 8 centimetres, are identical in appearance.

Precis lavinia

Precis (Junonia) lavinia

Precis lavinia is found in tropical America and the whole of the United States of America. The butterfly has a distinctive way of flying in which short gliding flights alternate with resting on the ground for short periods. The host plants of *Precis lavinia* are plantain and sedum. The butterfly hibernates in the colder parts of its distribution area.

Precis lemonias

Precis (Junonia) lemonias

Precis lemonias can be found in Sri Lanka, India, Pakistan and Burma. It is a very common butterfly which can be found up to a height of 2,500 metres. In Sri Lanka, this butterfly flies in large swarms at certain times. It is a migratory butterfly. Unlike most of the *Precis* species, it mainly lives in forests. It flies very fast and frequently lands on flowers to drink nectar. There is no difference in appearance between the males and the females of this species. Caterpillars live on plants belonging to the Acanthaceae family.

Precis octavia octavia

Precis octavia sesamus

Precis octavia

Precis octavia is one of the African representatives of the *Precis* genus. There is a lot of confusion about the naming of butterfly species in this genus because a lot of butterflies from other parts of the world which also belong to this genus are included in the related *Junonia* species. Two clearly distinguishable forms of *Precis octavia* are known, both of these are characteristic for the season. *Precis octavia octavia* belongs to the dry season, while *Precis octavia sesamus* belongs to the wet season. Both forms differ so much from each other in the pattern of colour on the upper sur-

face of the wings that they used to be considered as two different species. In addition, the underside of the butterfly from the dry season looks more like a dead leaf than the butterfly from the wet season. This butterfly has two generations a year in most parts of Africa. The caterpillar's host plants are coleus, plectranthus, iboza and other species of the Labiatae family. Towards evening, *Precis octavia* flies to a common sleeping place to spend the night with a large number of other butterflies of the same species.

Precis orythia

Precis (junonia) orythia

Precis orythia has a very large distribution area. It can be found in Africa, throughout Southeast Asia and in Australia. It is a common butterfly which flies from sea level to a height of more than 2,500 metres. In the lower lying areas, it is active throughout the year. In areas at a higher altitude, it is only active in the spring. It has a strong preference for hot and dry areas. They fly in the blazing sun and also sit on rocks in the full sun and on hot sand. Males go to muddy places to suck up water and undissolved minerals. Males and females visit lots of flowers to drink nectar. The caterpillars live on antirrhinum, angelonia and buchnera (Scrophulariaceae) and on *Thunbergia alata, Hygrophila salicifolia, Asystasia* and *Pseuderanthemum* (Acanthaceae). *Precis orythia* has a wingspan of 4 to 6 centimetres. The

Precis orythia

colours and markings on the upper surfaces of the wings are quite consistent, but can vary quite considerably on the undersides of the wings. Because of this variation, many subspecies of this widespread *Precis* species are known.

Vanessa atalanta

Vanessa atalanta, Red Admiral, can be found in Europe, Asia and North America. In Europe, it is a migratory butterfly originating from the Mediterranean, which flies up to the northern parts of Europe after the winter. About the time that it arrives in the Netherlands, thistles and stinging nettles are abundant. So, not only is there enough to drink on the flowers of thistles, which are rich in nectar, but the stinging nettles, which serve as host plants to lay eggs on, also have lots of leaves. The caterpillars of the Red Admiral live on their own and it takes about a month before they are ready to pupate. In the autumn, lots of these but-terflies can be seen in gardens, on the flowers of buddleia, asters and sedum. They also like the juices of rotting pears and plums, which have fallen from fruit trees. They disappear quite suddenly and make the long trek back to the south.

Vanessa atalanta, *Red Admiral*

Purple Emperors

Apatura ilia, *Small Purple Emperor*

Apatura iris, *Purple Emperor*

Apatura ilia

Apatura iris

Apatura ilia

Apatura ilia, Small Purple Emperor, can be found in an area stretching from Western Europe to the eastern part of Asia. Unlike *Apatura iris,* it prefers areas where the summers are a bit warmer. The butterflies drink the juices of rotting plants and overripe fruit. The caterpillar's host plants are poplars and willows. The immature caterpillars hibernate on these trees. Some stay in the cracks in the bark and others attach themselves to a bud by spinning a thread. The Small Purple Emperor only has one generation a year. In the warmer regions of its distribution area, there is a second generation. The butterflies have a preference for open spaces in woods or near edges of smaller woods especially the ones situated near riverbanks.

Apatura iris

Apatura iris, Purple Emperor, can be found from Western Europe to the eastern part of Asia. The butterfly gets its name from the unusual light-sensitive colours on its wings. Depending on the angle from which the sunlight shines on its wings, the colour changes from brown to dazzling blue. The butterflies drink a variety of juices: the juices of rotting fruit, sap seeping from trees, manure and even dead animals. Purple Emperors lay their eggs on various willow species (Salicaceae). The wonderfully camouflaged green caterpillars feed on the leaves. In autumn when the leaves turn brown, the caterpillars also change colour. These brown caterpillars hibernate in the fork of a branch. In the spring, the immature caterpillars carry on growing until they pupate in May. There is one brood a year. The butterflies fly in July.

Callicore cynosura, *ventral surface*

Callicore cynosura, *dorsal surface*

Callicore cynosura

Callicore cynosura is a typical representative of the South American genus *Callicore*, which also used to be called *Catagramma*. The red colour on the upper surface of the wings serves as a warning to frighten away enemies. The undersides of the fore-wings have the same markings, but they are orange coloured. The underside of the hind-

Callicore hydaspes, *dorsal surface*

wings has an unusual marking in which the letters 'a' and 'B' can be distinguished. *Callicore cynosura* has a wingspan of 5.5 to 6 centimetres.

Callicore hydaspes, *ventral surface*

Callicore hydaspes

The distribution area of *Callicore hydaspes* is restricted to Paraguay and the neighbouring parts of Brazil. Both males and females drink the juices of rotting fruit and the moisture in manure. Only the males drink the water and the undissolved minerals in wet sand. This is the only time that they land on the ground, otherwise they usually soar around the treetops in the rain forest. *Callicore hydaspes* is a relatively small representative of this genus with its wingspan of 4 to 4.5 centimetres. The caterpillars, which eat plants in the Sapindaceae family, have lots of spines on their dorsal surface and large branched outgrowths on their heads that look like antlers.

Callicore pitheas

Callicore pitheas lives in the area stretching from Mexico to Venezuela and Ecuador. The butterfly flies in dry forests at sea level and up to a height of 1,200 metres. This butterfly can usually be found near forest tracks and in open spaces in the full sun. In the rainy season, it flies in large numbers. However, in the dry season, hardly any butterflies can be found. The wingspan of this butterfly is 5 to 6 centime-

Callicore pytheas, *ventral surface*

Charaxes ameliae

tres. *Callicore pitheas* has lots of red markings on the upper surface of the wings, a colour which probably warns predators that this butterfly species is inedible. The caterpillar's host plants are plants belonging to the Sapindaceae family.

Callicore sorana, *ventral surface*

Callicore sorana

Callicore sorana lives in the forests of Brazil, Paraguay and Bolivia. This butterfly mainly flies near rivers and streams. Even though lots of butterflies in the *Callicore* genus are collected for the extraordinary markings on the underside of the hind-wings, not much is known about the immature stages. On the underside of the hind-wings, various numbers containing 0, 6 or 8 can be spotted on the beautiful markings. *Callicore sorana* has the number '80' unmistakably on the underside of its hind-wings. The wingspan of this butterfly is 5 to 6 centimetres.

Charaxes ameliae

Charaxes ameliae can be found in an area from the western part of Africa to Malawi and Uganda. The habitat of this butterfly is the forest where it drinks fermenting sap seeping from damaged trees. Especially in the wet season from May to June, a lot of these butterflies can be spotted. The pupa of *Charaxes ameliae* is very well camouflaged, because it is nearly impossible to distinguish it from the real gooseberry-like fruits growing on the bushes. The butterfly has a wingspan of 8 to 9 centimetres. Only the males have the shiny blue spotted pattern on the upper surface of the wings. The females have white spots.

Charaxes bohemani

Charaxes bohemani

Charaxes bohemani lives in southern parts of Africa, Zambia, Malawi, Zaire, Kenya and Botswana. It is an inhabitant of savannahs with lots of bushes and of wooded areas with lots of open spaces. It does not like dense forests. The host plants of the caterpillar are afzelia (Leguminosae) and sorghum (Graminae). The size of this butterfly species varies. The wingspan varies from 7.5 to 10.5 centimetres. *Charaxes bohemani* is easy to recognise because of the blue and black colours on the upper surface of the wings. Only the females have the distinctive white band right across the upper surface of the fore-wings.

Charaxes eupale

The distribution area of *Charaxes eupale* stretches from Sierra Leone in the western part of Africa up to Kenya. It is a typical forest butterfly feeding on the juices of fermenting fruit and on other rotting parts of plants. It is a relatively small *Charaxes* with a wingspan of 5.5 to 6 centimetres. The females are usually larger than the males. *Charaxes eupale*

has a beautiful dark-green camouflaging pattern on the underside of the wings. When resting the butterfly holds its wings together vertically above its body and is almost invisible.

Charaxes eurialus, *dorsal surface*

Charaxes eurialus

Charaxes eurialus can only be found on the Moluccas. It is one of the few *Charaxes* species that can be found outside of Africa. It is a powerful flyer and its appearance is characteristic for this

Charaxes eupale

Charaxes eurialus, *ventral surface*

butterfly genus. It has quite a large, thick body and wide square-shaped forewings. Small tails are attached to the hind-wings. The beautiful colours on the upper surfaces of the wings are also on the underside, only the pattern on the underside is much more elaborate and refined. The butterflies hardly ever visit flowers, but drink sap from rotting fruit and sap oozing from trees. In muddy places, the males drink water containing undissolved minerals. They are also able to secrete a drop of water from their proboscis to dissolve salts which they then suck up with the drop of water.

Charaxes jasius

Charaxes jasius

The female of *Charaxis jasius* has a wingspan of more than 8 centimetres and because of this is one of the largest butterflies in the *Nymphalidae* family. The upper surface of this butterfly is brown

with a pale orange edge, but the underside of the wings are covered with a beautiful pattern of colours. *Charaxis jasius* can be found in the Mediterranean area and in a large part of tropical Africa. The host plant of the caterpillars is the strawberry tree (Ericaceae). Males drink water from quagmires, both sexes love the juices of rotting fruit. Sometimes they drink so much of it that they become too heavy or too intoxicated to be able to fly properly.

Charaxes polyxena

Charaxes polyxena

Charaxes polyxena is an Asian *Charaxes*, which can be found in Sri Lanka, India, Pakistan and Burma. The butterfly lives in rain forests, where it flies around the treetops most of the time. The butterfly is not very discerning in its choice of host plant because the caterpillars feed on the plants belonging to a variety of families, such as *Annonaceae, Meliaceae* and *Leguminosae. Charaxes polyxena* is a large representative of the genus. The wingspan varies from 9 to 11.5 centimetres. Many subspecies of this *Charaxis* are known. Males of this butterfly species have two tails on the hind-wings, females only have one.

Charaxes smaragdalis

Charaxis smaragdalis is common in the western part of Africa, from Sierra Leone to Ghana. It is a powerful flyer which makes regular gliding flights. It feeds on

the juices of rotting fruit. The wingspan of both males and females is 8 centimetres. The colour on the upper surface of the wings is an important way of distinguishing between the sexes. The blue on the males is much darker and more shiny than that of the females.

Colobura dirce, *Mosaic*

Colobura dirce

Colobura dirce, the Mosaic Butterfly, is the only representative of this butterfly genus. It can be found in Mexico, Central America and in the northern part of South America. It is a fast flyer and lays its eggs on milkweed (*Asclepiadaceae*). The caterpillar feeds on the host plant from within a protective silken shell which it spins. The butterflies have extraordinary eyes on the tails and markings at the base of the wing which look like a zebra.

Euxanthe wakefieldi

Euxanthe wakefieldi can be found in the eastern and southeastern parts of Africa. The butterfly prefers to fly in shady places where it is difficult to spot due to its black and white pattern of colours. The white markings on the wings of the males have a greenish sheen when the sun shines on them. The females do not have this sheen. The host plant of the caterpillar is deinbollia. The caterpillar has a strong headpiece which is decorated with two small and two big horns.

Hypolimnas bolina

Hypolimnas bolina lives in India, Pakistan, Southeast Asia and Australia. The males have white markings on their wings which turn purple if the sun shines on them from the right angle. The males are identical throughout the distribution area. The females, however, vary quite a

Hypolimnas bolina

Hypolimnas dexithea

Hypolimnas bolina, *female*

bit from area to area. Some imitate poisonous butterflies belonging to the genus *Euploea*. The caterpillars of *Hypolimnas bolina* are not very fussy. They eat plants belonging to the *Acanthaceae, Amaranthaceae, Polygoniaceae* and *Rutaceae* families.

Hypolimnas dexithea

Unlike the other butterfly species in this genus, *Hypolimnas dexithea* has a very

Hypolimnas bolina

small distribution area. It can only be found on Madagascar and then only in the wooded areas in the north of the island. It is also unique because of the markings on its wings. The upper and underside are almost identical.

Hypolimnas misippus

Hypolimnas misippus

Hypolimnas misippus can be found in India and Pakistan, Australia, South America and North America. Not many butterflies have such a large distribution area. The differences in appearance in this large area are minute. The males of this butterfly look like the males of *H. bolina* and the females are an imitation of butterflies in the genus *Danaus*. Because this genus is poisonous, the females of *Hypolimnas misippus* also get left alone by predators.

Kallima inachus

Kallima inachus *drinking dew*

Kallima inachus

Kallima inachus can be found in India, Pakistan, Burma, China and Taiwan. The butterfly flies very rapidly through the rain forests, where it can usually be found near riverbanks. It feeds on the juices of rotting fruit. The host plants are girardinia (Urticaceae) and strobilanthus (Acanthaceae). The upper surface of the wings is a shiny blue with an orange band. The underside, on the other hand, is brown and looks exactly like a dry leaf, with a midrib and all. The tail on the hind-wings represents the stem of the leaf. Because of this *Kallima* species are also called leaf butterflies.

Lexias adonia

Lexias (Euthalia) adonia can be found on the islands of Java, Sumatra and Borneo in Indonesia. The butterflies live in rain forests where they fly along tracks and rivers. They mainly feed on the

Lexias adonia

Lexias dirtea, *male*

juices of rotting fruit. The wingspan of this butterfly varies between 5 and 7 centimetres. Females are quite a bit larger than males. The females also have a wide band of white markings across the middle of the fore- and hind-wings which the males do not have.

Lexias dirtea

Lexias dirtea, formerly known as *Euthalia dirtea*, can be found in India, Pak-istan, Burma, Malaysia and Indonesia. There is a big difference in appearance of the males and females of this butterfly. The male is black with a blue band along the edge of the hind-wings. The female is much larger and is a dark-brown colour with lots of yellow spots. It is a inhabitant of jungles where it flies along tracks and the edges of the forest. Males like to drink the juice of rotting pineapples.

LLexias dirtea, *female*

Lexias phemius

Lexias (Euthalia) phemius lives in a large part of Southeast Asia, from Burma to Hong Kong. Both males and females drink the juices of rotting fruit and suck up water with undissolved minerals from wet sand and mud. Females have been found with a wingspan of more than 6 centimetres, males are usually no more than 4 centimetres. The females can be recognised by the white band going diagonally over the fore-wings, males have a band of blue sheen on the edge of the hind-wings.

Limenitis camilla, *White Admiral*

Limenitis camilla

Limenitis camilla, White Admiral, is an inhabitant of woodlands in the temperate regions of Europe and Asia. The butterflies drink nectar from flowers and also the sap of various species of rotting plants. The host plant of the caterpillar is

honeysuckle (Caprifoliaceae). The immature caterpillar hibernates in a cocoon, which it makes on a branch of the host plant. There is one brood of White Admirals a year.

Neptis sappho

Neptis sappho

Nephtis sappho has a distribution area that stretches from Eastern Europe to the eastern part of Asia. It flies in the temperate regions in May and June and in the warmer regions it also flies in August and September. Its host plant is Lathyrus (Leguminoseae). It is a small butterfly with a wingspan of about 4 centimetres. It is a typical representative of a genus of various butterfly species which all look very much alike. They have a black and white marking on the upper surface of the wings and a yellow-white pattern of stripes on the underside. *Neptis* butterflies have an unusual way of flying. During flight they hold their wings out horizontally and glide for a short while.

Parthenos sylvia

Parthenos sylvia lives in Southeast Asia, from India to Malaysia and also in New Guinea. The colour on the upper surface of the wings varies from region to region and can, in addition to brown, be green, blue and even orange. The white markings are places where there are no colour scales and are therefore transparent. The

Parthenos sylvia, *blue form*

Parthenos sylvia

Salamis anactus

host plant of the caterpillar is adenia (Passifloraceae). *Parthenos sylvia* lives in forests and usually flies high above the treetops. Sometimes very large numbers of this butterfly gather on riverbanks to suck up water from the wet sand.

Salamis anactus

Salamis anactus is a typical representative of this genus of pearly white butterflies which are nearly entirely restricted to Africa. These butterflies have a dis-

tinctively white dorsal surface with small violet-coloured eye-spots, while the colouring and markings on the ventral surface look like a leaf. The lobe at the top of the fore-wings and the tail on the hind-wings contribute to this resemblance of a leaf. The wingspan is 8 to 9 centimetres.

Salamis duprei

Salamis duprei is only found on Madagascar. The host plants of the caterpillars

Salamis duprei

Salamis duprei

Salamis parhassus

Salamis parhassus

Salamis parhassus, Mother of Pearl, has a distribution area which covers all of tropical Africa south of the Sahara. It is a common butterfly in forests and dense shrubby areas. It often sits in between leaves and every now and again it makes short flights. The host plants of this caterpillar are plant species belonging to the *Asystadia* and *Isoglossa* (Acanthaceae) genera. The butterfly has a wingspan of 7.5 to 10 centimetres. The appearance of both sexes is identical. Their appearance does, however, vary according to the season. Butterflies from the wet season are darker and smaller and the lobe on their fore-wing is much smaller than that of the butterflies from the dry season.

Siproeta epaphus

are plants in the Acanthaceae family. When resting, *Salamis duprei* holds both its wings together vertically above its body. Due to the marvellous camouflaging colours on the underside of the wings it looks exactly like a leaf on a tree.

Siproeta epaphus

Siproeta epaphus can be found in an area stretching from Mexico to Peru. The butterfly flies in tropical rain forests that are situated at high altitudes. At about a distance of one to two metres above the ground, it patrols along the edges of the forest and searches for lantana flowers. Males and females drink nectar but only the males drink water and undissolved minerals from moist sand. *Siproeta epaphus* lays eggs in groups on the young leaves of ruellia and acanthus (Acanthaceae). The caterpillar has three spines on each segment and also has two horns on its head.

Siproeta stelenes

Siproeta stelenes, *ventral surface*

Siproeta stelenes

Siproeta stelenes can be found from the southern part of the United States of America up to the Amazon area. In Central America, it is one of the most common

Siproeta stelenes

butterflies. It likes to fly in the blazing sun and not only searches for flowers, but also for the sap of rotting fruit, manure and dead animals. The host plants of the caterpillar are ruellia and acanthus (Acanthaceae). *Siproeta stelenes* is very similar to the poisonous butterflies of the *Heliconius* family, a good example of mimicry.

Telchinia violae

Telchinia violae

Telchinia violae is a small butterfly from Sri Lanka and India. The wingspan is less than 3 centimetres. Males and females are difficult to distinguish from each other. The host plants of the caterpillars are plants of the Cucurbitaceae and Passifloraceae families. *Telchinia violae* is not a fast flyer, but it is a migratory butterfly which lives on Sri Lanka.

Vindula arsinoe, *female*

Vindula *male*

Vindula arsinoe

The distribution area of *Vindula arsinoe* stretches from Malaysia to the northern part of Australia. The butterflies live in the rain forest. The females usually fly up high, the males come down to the ground to visit flowers. Lantana is a special favourite. The males also drink the juices from dead animals and from the dung of mammals and birds. When they suck up water and undissolved salts from wet sand, they also secrete drops of fluid from their abdomen. This fluid is probably mainly water and is used to wet the sand so that they are able to dissolve the salts again. The females lay one egg at a time on the tendril of the host plant. The host plants of the caterpillars are *Adenia heterophylla* and *Passiflora aurantia* (Passifloraceae). The wingspan of the males of *Vindula arsinoe* is no more than 7.5 centimetres, but that of the females can be as large as 9 centimetres. The colours on the wings of both sexes are very different.

Argynnis paphia, *Silver-washed Fritillary*

Vindula erota

Vindula erota can be found in India, Pakistan, Burma, Thailand, Malaysia and Indonesia. It is quite a common butterfly in open spaces and in jungles. They like to visit lantana flowers to drink nectar. The caterpillar's host plants are the many species of passiflora (Passifloraceae). The yellow and brown-coloured caterpillar has spines all over its body and has a pair of horns on its head. The pupa looks like a shrivelled up, dry leaf and is hardly recognisable as a pupa. The butterfly has a wingspan of 7 to 9.5 centimetres. A white band runs along the side of the wide orange-brown band at the base of the fore- and hind-wings. The hind-wings have a tail.

Argynnis paphia valesina

Fritillaries

Argynnis paphia

Arginnis paphia, Silver-washed Fritillary, is a large Fritillary which flies from the northern part of Africa and Europe up to eastern Asia. Male Silver-washed Fritillaries can be recognised by the scent strips on the upper side of the fore-wings. Apart from the red-brown variety of this butterfly, there is also a dark-brown one: *forma valesina*. The Silver-washed Fritillary flies in woods and parks where their host plants, various violet species (Violaceae), grow. As soon as the caterpillars hatch out, they crawl away into cracks in the bark of a tree growing near the violets. Here they can hibernate in safety. Butterflies of this species can reach an age of more than seven weeks.

Boloria aquilonaris, *Cranberry Fritillary*

Boloria aquilonaris

Boloria aquilonaris, Cranberry Fritillary, can only be found on moorland in Europe and western Asia. The name of this butterfly comes from the caterpillar's main host plant, the cranberry (Ericaceae).

The caterpillars of the Cranberry Fritillary hibernate hidden away in the peat moss.

After about two months, the caterpillars are fully grown and pupate. The butterflies, which emerge from the pupae, fly in

Chlosyne janais

July. There is only one generation a year of this very rare Fritillary.

Brenthis daphne, *Marble Fritillary*

Brenthis daphne

Brenthis daphne, Marble Fritillary, has a distribution area spread over the whole of Europe and Asia. The butterfly lays its eggs on blackberry bushes (Rosaceae). Preferably blackberry bushes on the edges of woods and on the banks of streams. The eggs, which are laid on old dry flowers, hibernate here. There is one generation a year, the butterflies of which fly in July.

Chlosyne janais

Chlosyne janais is a small butterfly which can be found in a distribution area from Mexico to Colombia. The main host plant is odontonema, but the caterpillars also eat other plants in the Acan-

thaceae family. The females of this butterfly lay their eggs in groups. When laid, the eggs are immediately ready to hatch. Recently fertilised females are so heavy that it is difficult for them to fly. Caterpillars from the same brood stay together in a group and feed on the same host plant. The butterflies fly in open areas and especially in the dry season they can be found in very large numbers. Males and females visit flowers regularly. When drinking they catch the eye, because they constantly move their wings.

Clossiana dia, *Violet Fritillary*

Clossiana dia

Clossiana dia, Violet Fritillary, can be found in the European and Asian steppes. The butterflies drink nectar from the flowers of herbs. They lay their eggs on various species of violet (Violaceae). The immature caterpillar of the Violet Fritillary hibernates in between the withered leaves in the leaf litter. In the spring, they grow

Clossiana dia

Clossiana selene, *Small Pearl-bordered Fritillary*

quickly and then pupate. The butterflies from this brood fly in May, those from the second brood fly in July and August.

Clossiana selene

Clossiana selene, Small Pearl-bordered Fritillary, can be found in the cool and wet regions of Europe, Asia and North America. Violets (Violaceae), the plants on which the butterflies lay their eggs, grow on peat moors, marshlands and wet grasslands. The immature caterpillar

hibernates in between the leaves of the leaf litter. In the spring, the caterpillar grows quickly, feeding on the fresh young violets. The butterflies that subsequently emerge from the chrysalis, fly in the period from June to July. Sometimes there is a second brood of Small Pearl-bordered Fritillaries.

Dynamine mylitta

Dynamine mylitta is a striking butterfly which has a distribution area stretching

Clossiana selene

Dynamine mylitta

search for violets (Violaceae), usually the field pansy, to lay eggs on. The immature caterpillar crawls in between the leaves in the leaf litter to hibernate in safety. There are two to three broods of the Queen of Spain Fritillary a year.

Melitaea cinxia, *Glanville Fritillary*

from Mexico to far into South America. The eggs are laid on plants in the Euphorbiaceae family. The caterpillars mainly eat buds, flowers and young leaves. When they are not eating, the caterpillars sit in the leaf axil and look identical to the flower buds. The butterflies fly in the blazing sun near the edges of forests where their host plant can be found. The females only fly short distances, even if they are not laying eggs. The males fly long distances to drink water from wet sand near riverbanks. They also feed on the moisture in the manure of mammals. Butterflies of both sexes like flowers from the Asteraceae family.

Issoria lathonia, *Queen of Spain Fritillar*

Issoria lathonia

Issoria lathonia, Queen of Spain Fritillary, can be found in a large part of North Africa, Europe and Asia. The butterflies feed on nectar from flowers. They

Melitaea cinxia

Melitaea cinxia, Glanville Fritillary, can be found in a distribution area throughout the warmer regions of Europe and Asia. The butterflies lay large numbers of eggs on the leaves of plantain plants (Plantaginaceae). The caterpillars stay together in large cocoon nests on the plant. Sometimes there can be 100 to 200 caterpillars in one these nests. After they have shed their skin a few of times, they make a cocoon in the leaf litter to hibernate in. In the spring, they feed on the young nutritious plantain, but they grow

Melitaea didyma, *Spotted Fritillary*

very slowly. It is not until June that the Glanville Fritillary flies in flowery grassland.

Melitaea didyma

Melitaea didyma

Melitaea didyma

Melitaea didyma, Spotted Fritillary, is found distributed throughout the hot to very hot regions of North Africa and Europe to as far as Central Asia. This butterfly searches for nectar in dry flowery fields. The caterpillar's host plants are various species of plantain (Plantaginaceae) and snapdragon (Scrophulariaceae). The caterpillars live together in groups of many dozens in one cocoon. The Spotted Fritillary hibernates as an immature caterpillar. There is one generation a year. The butterflies fly in July.

Mellicta athalia

Mellicta athalia, Heath Fritillary, is found spread throughout a large part of Europe and Asia. It prefers to live on the edges of woods and in open areas. Various plantain species (Plantaginaceae)

Mellicta athalia, *Heath Fritillary*

Mellicta athalia

and figwort species (Scrophulariaceae) are the host plants of the caterpillars. The butterfly lays dozens of eggs on these plants. The caterpillars stay together in cocoon nests on the host plant. The immature caterpillar hibernates. In the spring, they grow quickly and pupate. There is one generation a year. The Heath Fritillary can be found locally in large numbers.

Mellicta britomartis

Mellicta britomartis, Assman's Fritillary, can be found in an area stretching from Germany and Eastern Europe to as far as the eastern part of Asia. The host plants are plants in the Plantaginaceae and Scrophulariaceae families. Sometimes the butterflies lay their eggs together in groups of more than a hundred on the plant. The caterpillars also stay together. They hibernate together in a cocoon, which they make in the leaf litter. In the spring, they continue to grow and then pupate. There is one generation

Mesoacidalia aglaja, *Dark-green Fritillary*

Mellicta britomatis, *Assman's Fritillary*

a year. Assman's Fritillary flies from the end of June to the beginning of August. With its wingspan of less than 2 centimetres it is one of the smallest fritillaries.

Mesoacidalia aglaja

Mesoacidalia aglaja, Dark-green Fritillary, has a distribution area which stretches from Western Europe up to the eastern part of Asia. The butterfly flies in a large variety of biotopes, such as grasslands, heaths, and marshlands, wherever violets (Violaceae) can be found. Various violet species are the host plants of the caterpillar. Females of the Dark-green Fritillary lay their eggs on the host plant. As soon as the caterpillars hatch out, they crawl into the leaf litter to hibernate. In the spring, they return to the young violets to feed. There is but one brood a year.

Greta oto

13 Small butterfly families

Acraeidae

Most of the butterflies in the Acraeidae family can be found in Africa. A few species live in tropical Southeast Asia and one genus lives in America. In Africa, there are more than 150 Acraea species. Some live in rain forests, others in deserts. The caterpillars of many species live on passifloraceous plants and because of this the caterpillars are poisonous. Lots of other butterflies imitate the appearance and behaviour of Acraeas.

Acraea egina

Acraea egina

Acraea egina can be found in a distribution area all over tropical Africa to the north of Zimbabwe and Mozambique. It lives in woods, where it usually flies at a height of two to three metres. It does not visit many flowers. The wingspan is 6 to 9 centimetres. It is a typical representative of a family of more than 150 species, which, with a few exceptions, all live in Africa. They are slow flyers with lots of red markings warning birds and other insect eaters that they are inedible. Many other butterfly species, for example *Graphium ridleyanus*, which are not poisonous, imitate the Acraea's col-

oration to warn off predators; a perfect example of mimicry.

Acraea encedon

Acraea encedon

Acraea encedon is a common butterfly in Africa in the region south of the equator. It prefers to fly along the banks of streams and rivers where reeds grow. They are tough butterflies which when caught sometimes secrete a yellow-coloured foamy fluid. This foam contains the very poisonous hydrocyanic acid. The butterfly does not get this poisonous substance from the host plant. The caterpillars' host plant is commelina. This plant is poisonous, but does not contain hydrocyanic acid. The butterfly produces this substance itself in its body. The colours on the wings of the butterfly are a warning against this poison. The coloration of *Acraea encedon* looks exactly like that of *Danaus chrysippus*. This is an unrelated butterfly, which can be found in the same region and is also inedible to birds and mammals. This form of mimicry, when two very similar butterflies are poisonous, is called Müllerian mimicry.

Acraea horta

Acraea horta is one of the most common butterflies in southern parts of Africa. The males catch the eye because of the red and black colours on the fore-wings, the females in contrast are light brown. The fore-wings of both sexes are almost transparent. The butterfly is active throughout the year. The host plant is *Kiggelaria africana*, a type of wild peach. This plant contains poisonous substances. The cater-pillars feed on this plant and because of this are also poisonous. They do not need to hide when danger threatens, because they can count on being left alone. Besides the fact that they are inedible, the caterpillars also have forked spines to frighten off predators. The colourful butterflies are also inedible.

Acraea hova

Acraea hova can only be found on Madagascar. The distribution area of the butterflies of the *Acraea* family is mainly restricted to the African continent. The caterpillars feed on poisonous plants belonging to the Aristolochiaceae and Apocynacea families. The butterfly is also poisonous to insect-eating birds. When in danger, it secretes a drop of yellow, distasteful fluid, which ends up in the mouth or beak of the attacker. The butterfly is immediately set free. Acraeas are such tough butterflies that they usually survive such rough treatment. Many butterflies imitate the appearance of this species.

Acraea hova

Acraea natalica

Acraea natalica

Acraea natalica can be found the part of Africa which is south of the equator, all the way down to the Cape in the far south. Throughout the year, this butterfly is common in wooded areas, savannahs and areas with low-growing shrubs. The butterfly has a characteristic shape having a long abdomen and narrow wings, but on the other hand varies a lot in the coloration on the wings. Within certain regions, the difference in colour depends on the season. The butterflies in the wet season are bright red in colour with pitch black markings, whereas in the dry season the butterflies are quite a bit smaller and are less brightly coloured.

Acraea zetes

Acraea zetes

Acraea zetes can be found almost throughout the whole of Africa, to the south of the Sahara. It is common in the savannahs and near the edges of wooded areas, but hardly ever flies in large numbers. The butterfly has a wingspan between 6 and 7.5 centimetres. It can be recognised by the distinctively coloured point on the abdomen and by the distinctive black bands on its wings. The female butterflies are brighter than the males. The host plants of the caterpillar are plants of the Passifloraceae family, such as passiflora species, moduca and adenia, all of which are poisonous plants. This poison makes both the yellow and black striped caterpillars and the butterflies inedible.

Ithomiidae

Butterflies from the Ithomiidae family are indigenous to Central and South America. Nearly all of them are live in forests. The caterpillars of most species live on the poisonous plants of the Solanaceae family. The butterflies are inedible to insect eaters. Their appearance, whether it is characterised by an orange, yellow and black striped pattern or by transparent wings, is imitated by many other butterfly species.

Dircenna dero

Dircenna dero

Dircenna dero can be found from Mexico to Brazil. The butterfly is found in forests from sea level to a height of 1,000 metres. It flies along rivers or in places where the sun shines through the foliage.

The butterfly can be seen throughout the year, but never flies in large numbers. In some seasons, it behaves like a migratory butterfly. Males and females visit inga, psychotria and lantana flowers. Males also sit on rotting plants such as senecio to extract alkaloids. They need this substance to make their pheromones. The host plant of *Dircenna dero* is *Solanum ochraceoferrugineum* (Solanaceae). The butterfly has a wingspan of 7 to 7.5 centimetres and can be recognised by its yellow antennae.

The caterpillar of Greta oto

Greta oto

Greta oto can be found from Mexico to Panama. The butterflies lay their eggs on various species of plants in the Cestrum genus, such as *C. lanatum* and *C. standleyi*. These plants belong to the Solanaceae family. The female lays one egg at a time and then searches for the next host plant. Sometimes she keeps coming back to the same plant, so in the end quite a few eggs can be laid on one plant. The pale caterpillars do not have any spines. *Greta oto* is a very common Clearwing Butterfly, which feels at home in a large variety of biotopes. It can be seen as a butterfly throughout the year; in some seasons it is present in very large numbers, but in other seasons, only a few individuals can be seen. The butterfly can fly very long distances in short periods of time. It is recorded that a *G.*

oto in Costa Rica had flown more than 40 kilometres in the space of 24 hours. On average, the butterflies fly about 12 kilometres a day.

Ithomia patilla

Ithomia patilla

The distribution area of *Ithomia patilla* stretches from Mexico to Panama. It is one of the most common Clearwing Butterflies in Central America. It is found from sea level to a height of 1,600 metres. Not only can it be found in wooded areas, but in all sorts of terrains because it migrates every now and again. Males and females visit the flowers of inga, lantana, hamelia, psychotria plants and many flowers in the Asteraceae family. The female lays her eggs on witheringia and lycianthes (Solanaceae). The caterpillar does not feed on the edge of the leaf, but eats holes in the leaf. When resting, it sitson the edge of the hole it has eaten in the leaf. The caterpillar and the butterfly are inedible to insect eaters.

Ithomia terra

Ithomia terra

Ithomia terra can be found in South America, from Costa Rica to Bolivia. It lives in forests on mountainsides at a height of 1,000 to 2,000 metres. It flies near to the ground and usually stays in the shade. Males come out of the jungle early in the morning to suck up alkaloids. At other times, it stays in the jungle. Unlike the other butterflies in the *Ithomia* genus, *Ithomia terra* does not show any migratory behaviour. It is quite a rare butterfly and not much is known about the immature stages. With a wingspan of 4.5 to 5 centimetres, it is a small *Ithomia* species.

Ithomia xenos

The distribution area of *Ithomia xenos* is restricted to Costa Rica and Panama in Central America. The butterfly inhabits rain forests growing at a height of 880 to 2,000 metres. Males and females mainly fly around the treetops and just below the foliage. They visit flowers of lantana plants in the lower regions and those of *Senecio megaphylla* higher up the mountains. The host plants of the caterpillars are species of *Witheringia* and *Acnistus* (Solanaceae). It is one of the few Clearwing Butterflies that has a yellow tint.

Mechanitis isthmia

Mechanitis isthmia

Mechanitis isthmia can be found from Mexico to the Amazon basin in South

Ithomia xenos

America. The butterfly stays in the forest when it is cloudy but when it is sunny, it comes out to visit flowers. It mainly drinks nectar from eupatorium flowers. The host plant of the caterpillar is solanum (Solanaceae). These plants contain poisonous substances which make both the caterpillars and the butterflies inedible. Both edible and poisonous butterflies imitate the coloration of this butterfly. A lot of butterfly species in various families look very much alike because of this mimicry.

Mechanitis menapis

Mechanitis menapis

The distribution area of *Mechanitis menapis* stretches from Mexico to Ecuador in South America. It lives in jungles situated on mountainsides at a height of 700 to 2,000 metres. Males and females visit inga, senecio and eupatorium flowers. The females usually search for host plants growing on the edges of forests early in the morning. The host plants of the caterpillars are *Solanum hispidum*, *Solanum torvum* and other plants of the *Solanum* genus (Solanaceae). With its wingspan of 7.5 to 8 centimetres, *Mechanitis menapis* is one of the largest butterflies in the genus *Mechanitis*.

Mechanitis polymnia

Mechanitis polymnia can be found from Mexico to the Amazon area in South

Mechanitis polymnia

America. It is the most common butterfly in the Ithomiidae family. It flies from sea level to a height of 1,500 metres. It has no preference for a specific biotope. Throughout the year, the butterfly flies in shady woods, in sunny open spaces and even cities and villages are not avoided. The female lays her eggs in groups of 10 to 40 on plants in the genus *Solanum* (Solanaceae). The caterpillars live together in large numbers without becoming cannibalistic. Many related and unrelated butterfly species have the same coloration and have remarkably complicated mimetic associations. *Mechanitis polymnia* has a wingspan of 6.5 to 7.5 centimetres.

Brassolidae

Butterflies in the Brassolidae family can only be found in the tropical parts of America. They are usually large butterflies with distinctive eye-spots on the underside of the hind-wings. Most of the species are active at dusk and dawn. The juices of rotting fruit is their main source of food.

Caligo atreus

Caligo atreus, which lives in the region from Mexico to Peru, is a large representative of the Noctuid Moth family. The butterfly can be easily recognised by the orange band across the wings. These

Caligo atreus

Mating of Caligo atreus

large butterflies have a distinctive courtship flight, in which they continuously circle around each other. After mating, the females lay their eggs on plants in the genus *Musa* and on heliconia. Because of this they can cause enormous damage to plantations where bananas, which also belong to the genus *Musa,* are grown. The eggs are always laid in small numbers. The caterpillars feed together and when they are not eating they form a kind of colony of caterpillars packed together. When they are a bit bigger, they lie along the midrib of the leaves. Towards evening, they come out and feed on the edge of the leaves and in the morning they can safely rest against the midrib again. The butterflies, which fly around at dusk and dawn, live on the juices of rotting fruit.

Caligo idomeneus

Caligo idomeneus can be found from the northern part of South America down to Argentina. It is a very large butterfly with

Caligo idomeneus

Caterpillar of Caligo memnon

Caterpillar of Caligo memnon

Caligo memnon

Caligo memnon is one of the most well-known Noctuid Moths (from the Latin *noctua* meaning night owl), and is found from Mexico to the Amazon area. They get their name from the striking eye-spots on the underside of their hind-wings. These eye-spots look like the eyes of an owl, and hence these moths are some-

a wingspan of 14 centimetres. The flash markings so characteristics of this genus are clearly visible on the underside of the hind-wings. It is a common butterfly, which flies early in the morning and in the evening. It feels at home in the jungle. Males and females drink the juices of rotting bananas. The females lay small groups of eggs on the leaves of the banana, (Musaceae). Sometimes the butterfly is a serious pest on banana plantations.

Caligo *on rotting banana*

Caligo memnon

202

times called owlet moths. These eyes serve to frighten off predators. Unlike the other Noctuid Moths, *C. memnon* is active throughout the year, even in the dry season. It does not really like the tropical rain forest, but loves the rainy season. This is when it usually flies in large numbers. The butterfly, which is active at dusk, feeds on the juices of rotting fruit. The especially large caterpillars have a very hard headpiece. In addition to this, the caterpillars secrete a substance that keeps even a colony of migratory ants away.

Caligo prometheus

Caligo prometheus

Caligo prometheus is found in Ecuador and Columbia in South America. With its wingspan of sometimes more than 15 centimetres, it is one of the largest Noctuid Moths. Males and females have the same coloration on the ventral and dorsal surfaces. At the top of the yellow-coloured fore-wings, there is a dark edge along the outer margin of the wing. The hind-wings are dark-brown with sometimes a pale and sometimes a bright blue sheen at the base.

Dynastor napoleon

Dynastor napoleon can only be found in the rain forests of Brazil. The butterfly is active in the morning and at dusk. Unlike the other butterflies of the Brassolidae family, this species does not drink the juices of rotting fruit. The

Dynastor napoleon

green caterpillars have a forked tail and a headpiece with a large number of hard spines on it. They live on plants of the Bromeliaceae family. The chrysalis has extraordinary markings, which look exactly like a snake's head, including the eyes and scales. The butterfly has a wingspan of 12 to 16 centimetres. The females are quite a bit larger than the males. Both sexes have the same coloration with a distinctive wide orange-coloured edge on the outer margin of the hind-wings. The underside of the hind-wing looks like a leaf with pronounced veins due to the dark marking of the veins on the wings.

Eryphanis polyxena, *ventral surface*

Eryphanis polyxena

Eryphanis polyxena can be found from Guatemala to the Amazon basin in Brazil. It inhabits rain forests situated up to a height of 1,200 metres. The butter-

Eryphanis polyxena, *dorsal surface*

flies fly in open spaces in the forests in the morning and at dusk. Males and females visit rotting fruit to drink the juices. The host plant is bamboo (Graminae). The caterpillars eat at night and during the day they lie against the stem of the bamboo plant and on the leaf bases of dead leaves. *Eryphanis polyxena* can be recognised for example by the markedly extended hind-wings. The butterflies have a wingspan of 8 to 10 centimetres. The upper surface of the wings of the males have a magnificent blue sheen and a yellow oval spot with scent-emitting scales on the inner margin of the hind-wings.

Opsiphanes cassina

Opsiphanes cassina is a small representative of the Brassolidae family, which can be found from Mexico to the Amazon area. The host plants of the caterpillar include the leaves of the coconut tree and of other palm trees. The caterpillars

Opsiphanes cassina

are light green in colour and have a forked tail. They lie alongside the vein of the palm leaf inside a shell which they make themselves. They gnaw off part of the leaf and wrap this around themselves. The structure is held together with a silken thread. Caterpillars like these are almost impossible to find. The butterflies do not visit flowers, but feed on the juices of rotting and overripe fruit. They are active at dusk. Because of their preference for coconut trees, the caterpillars are controlled on plantations.

Opsiphanes tamarindi

Opsiphanes tamarindi

Opsiphanes tamarindi

rotting fruit such as bananas and mangoes. They also drink moisture from dung. They search for this at night near houses and even in villages. The female chiefly lays its eggs on the stems and dead leaves of the host plant. Heliconia and banana (Musaceae) are the caterpillar's main host plants. On both banana plantations and in the rain forest, the caterpillars are preyed on by ichneumon wasps and parasite flies. With a wingspan of less than 10 centimetres, Opsiphanes tamarindi is a relatively small butterfly of the Brassolidae family.

Opsiphanes tamarindi

Opsiphanes tamarindi lives from Mexico to the Amazon area in South America. The butterflies mainly fly in forest situated on mountainsides up to a height of 1,200 metres. They feed on the juices of

Morphidae

The butterflies of the Morphidae family belong to the most spectacular butterflies in the world. They are large and have a beautiful blue sheen on their wings. They live in the rain forests in the tropical

Morpho aega, *male*

Morpho aega, *female*

parts of America. The butterflies only feed on the juices of rotting fruit and do not visit flowers.

Morpho aega

Morpho aega is a wonderful example of a butterfly with the metallic blue colours characteristic of the genus Morpho. It is a very common sight in Brazil. Millions of specimens of this butterfly species are caught every year to be made into jewellery and paintings to sell to tourists. Only the bright blue males are used for this. Because of this, in spite of all the captures, the species is not endangered with extinction. The fact that the caterpillars' host plant, the bamboo plant *Chusquea*, grows abundantly in a large part of Brazil, also plays an important part in this. The females of *Morpho aega* have an orange and brown underlying colour with yellow-coloured markings,

sometimes covered with a light blue sheen. The wingspan is usually no more than 10 centimetres.

Morpho cypris, *dorsal surface*

Morpho cypris

Morpho cypris lives from Nicaragua in Central America to Columbia. The butterfly is an inhabitant of rain forests situated on mountainsides up to a height of about 1,000 metres. Males are most active when the sun has reached its highest point, between 10.30 a.m. and 1 p.m. At this time of the day, the blue on their wings is exceptionally bright because of the angle at which the sun shines on them. The wingspan of the males is about 12 centimetres. The females of *Morpho cypris* are quite a bit larger. Their wingspan can be as much as 16 centimetres. The females have dull orange-coloured wings. When the female has found an appropriate host plant she

Morpho cypris, *ventral surface*

only lays one egg on it and goes off to search for the next plant. She often keeps coming back to the same plant and ends up laying a large number of eggs on one plant. The host plant of this butterfly species is *Inga marginata* (Mimosaceae). The caterpillars secrete a drop of clear fluid from a gland at the top of their thorax. They spread this fluid all over the bristles on their head. The smell possibly keeps away other caterpillars of the same sort if there are too many on one plant.

Morpho deidamia

Morpho deidamia has a distribution area which stretches from Guyana in the northern part of South America to the Amazon area. It is a fast, strong flyer which lives near the edges of forests and riverbanks in the tropical rain forests of the region. On the upper side of the wings, the butterfly has a wide band of

Morpho deidamia, *dorsal surface*

Morpho deidamia, *ventral surface*

blue sheen. The underside has a brown pattern of markings with eye-shaped structures. The large difference in colour between the upper and underside of the wings is important to confuse possible predators. A bird chasing this species of Morpho first sees a blue and then a brown butterfly. Because of this, it can not keep track of its prey properly and so the butterfly has the chance to escape.

Morpho laertes

Morpho laertes

Morpho laertes is an eye-catching, white butterfly, which lives in the rain forests of Brazil. Both males and females of this species have a beautiful pearly sheen on their wings. Females lay their eggs on plants of the genus *Inga* (Mimosaceae). The caterpillars live together in large numbers in cocoon nests in the trees.

Morpho menelaus

Morpho menelaus is found widely spread throughout the rain forests of South America. Throughout the year, it flies along the edges of forests and in open spaces in the forests. The butterfly is active from early in the morning up to the time that the sun reaches its highest point in the sky. The wingspan is 13 to 14 centimetres. However, the body of this butterfly is only small. During a normal flight, the butterfly does not beat its

Morpho menelaus orinocoensis

wings very often and mainly glides through the air. When in danger, *Morpho menelaus* shoots off suddenly beating its powerful wings very quickly and it is very hard for predators to catch. This butterfly species lays its eggs on plants of the genus *Erythroxylum*.

Morpho peleides

Morpho peleides is a distinctive sight in Mexico, Central America, Columbia and Venezuela. The butterfly's host plants are mucuna, dalbergia and pterocarpus, all plants in the Fabaceae family. The caterpillars are adorned with colourful bunches of hair. The caterpillars have glands near their front pair of legs from which they can secrete a disgusting smelling substance when attacked. The underside of the butterfly's wings is brown with eyespots. The upper surface of the wings of the female is brown and that of the males is predominantly blue. The iridescent blue on some of the subspecies is restricted to a narrow band, while on others the

Caterpillar of Morpho peleides

Morpho peleides, *dorsal surface*

Morpho peleides, *ventral surface*

Morpho perseus

Morpho perseus is found from Central America to Venezuela and Brazil in South America. Unlike most of the other Morphos, this butterfly species is not blue at all or hardly at all, but is predominantly brown. This is the case in both males and females. The wingspan of *Morpho perseus* is 12 to 14 centimetres.

Morpho polyphemus

Morpho polyphemus can be found from Mexico to Costa Rica. It is a distinctive butterfly in the Morpho genus because it is pure white and not shiny blue. Males usually soar around the treetops and along tracks and riverbanks. They constantly hunt down males of their own kind. They do the same to other large white butterflies, for example to mem-

Morpho polyphemus

whole of the upper side of the wings is a beautiful blue. The butterfly is a conspicuous flyer along edges of forests and riverbanks. It feeds on the juices of rotting fruit and sap seeping from damaged trees. When it drinks, it holds its wings folded together above its body. In this way, the blue colour does not show and the butterflies are inconspicuous.

Morpho perseus

bers of the Whites family. Both sexes usually actively search for food in the morning. Their main preference is rotting fruit.

Morpho portis, *female*

Morpho portis

Morpho portis lives locally in the forests of Brazil and Uruguay. With a wingspan of almost 9 centimetres it is one of the smaller Morpho species. The largest, *Morpho hecuba*, is nearly three times as big. Males and females of *Morpho portis*

barely differ in appearance. They mainly fly in the late afternoon, usually near to the ground. They search for fallen, rotting fruit, which is the butterfly's main food.

Morpho rhetenor

Morpho rhetenor is a distinctive inhabitant of the rain forests of the northern part of South America in countries such as Colombia, Peru, Venezuela, Ecuador and Surinam. The bright blue males are

Morpho rhetenor augustina, *dorsal surface*

Morpho rhetenor casica

Morpho rhetenor augustina, *ventral surface*

Morpho theseus

very striking when they patrol along forest tracks and riverbanks and when they fly around the treetops. The much less strikingly-coloured females hardly show themselves and stay inside the forest. The caterpillars' host plant is *Macrolobium bifolium*. The butterflies do not drink nectar, but love the juices of rotting fruit. They also like the sap oozing from places where trees are damaged and which ferments after a while. While drinking, they hold their wings folded together above their body. In this way the butterfly is very inconspicuous because of the brown pattern of markings on the underside of the wings. Many subspecies can be found in the various parts of the distribution area, they can be distinguished by the pattern of white markings on the blue colour of the wings. *Morpho rhetenor* is one of the largest representatives of the genus *Morpho*. Its wingspan can be larger than 15 centimetres.

Morpho theseus

Morpho theseus is found in Mexico, the whole of Central America and in the northern part of South America down to Peru. It inhabits rain forests which are found from sea level to a height of 2,000 metres. Males fly high up above the treetops near canyons and rivers. Early in the morning, they are active near open spaces in the rain forest. During the courtship flights the male dances above

and behind the female for long distances to seduce her into mating. An unusual threat to this Morpho is a species of parasitic fly, the larvae of which live in the abdomen of the females of this butterfly.

Danaidae

The Danaidae or Monarchs form a family of more than 300 species, which mainly live in the tropics and subtropics. The shape of the wings and the wing markings of dark lines are almost identical in most of the species. There is, however, quite a difference in size. Their wingspan varies from 5 to 18 centimetres. All of the species have poisonous substances in their bodies. The caterpillars eat poisonous plants and store these poisonous substances in their body. The more poisonous the plant the caterpillar eats, the more distasteful the butterfly is to insect eaters. The Monarchs give the warning

Amauris rashti

Danaus plexippus *on* Asclepias

that they are inedible by the distinctive coloration on their wings. Many Monarchs, and especially *Danaus plexippus*, the Monarch after which the whole family is named, are migratory butterflies.

an inhabitant of very humid forests. The host plants of the caterpillar include cyanchum and tylophora, both poisonous plants of the Asclepiadaceae family. The butterfly is inedible to predators such as birds. Many subspecies of this *Amauris* species are known. Many of these subspecies serve as a model imitated by edible butterflies. Some of the females of *Papilio dardanus*, which live in the same area, as well as a related species such as *Amauris echeria*, look exactly like this butterfly species. The width of the yellow band on the hind-wings and the colour of the spots on the fore-wings are characteristic. *Amauris albimaculata* has a wingspan of 6 to 8 centimetres.

Amauris albimaculata

Amauris albimaculata

Amauris albimaculata lives in a large part of Africa, south of the Sahara. It is

Amauris echeria

Amauris echeria lives in the tropical parts of Africa stretching from Central Africa to South Africa. This butterfly varies a lot in appearance, so there are many subspecies. Some of these are

Amauris echeria

identical to a related species. The subspecies shown here is indistinguishable from *Amauris albimaculata*. The males and females of *Amauris echeria* are identical in each region. The butterflies fly throughout most of the year. The host plants of the caterpillar are plants in the *Tylophora*, *Secamona* and *Marsdenia* genera.

Amauris niavius

Amauris niavius

Amauris niavius is found in the tropical and subtropical parts of Africa. This butterfly lives in the forest. The butterfly drinks nectar and feeds on the moisture in dung. The butterfly is inedible and for this reason serves as a model for many edible butterflies such as *Papilio dardanus* and *Hypolimnas*. Many subspecies of *Amaurus niavius* are known, and the main difference between the subspecies is the size of the white markings on the

wings. With its wingspan of 8 to 11.5 centimetres, this *Amauris* species is one of the largest representatives of the genus.

Danaus chrysippus

Danaus chrysippus

The Plain Tiger, *Danaus chrysippus*, has a very large distribution area. From the Canary Islands through Africa, the Middle East, Southeast Asia to New Guinea and Australia. It occasionally visits Europe too. The butterflies are found in various kinds of climates. In the tropics, the caterpillar grows so fast that there are as many as twelve broods a year. In other areas, the number of broods is restricted to one or two a year. The host plants usually belong to the *Calotropis* genus, but other members of the Asclepiadaceae are also eaten. The coloration of *D. chrysippus* is imitated by many other butterfly species. A wonderful example is *Hypolimnas misippus*, which occurs in two colours. Both these forms imitate two different subspecies of *D. chrysippus*.

Danaus plexippus

Danaus plexippus, Monarch, is found in the tropical and subtropical regions all over the world. The migration of this butterfly in North America is the most well-known example of a migratory butterfly. Monarchs hibernate together in enormous numbers; tens of millions of Monarch butterflies hibernate in a small

Danaus plexippus, *drinking water*

Danaus plexippus, *hibernating*

number of forests in California and especially in Mexico. At the end of winter, the butterflies fly northwards. In many places they find fresh young *Asclepias* plants, which have just germinated and flowered. The butterflies drink a lot of nectar from the flowers of this plant and then they lay their eggs on the leaves. The main nectar plant is therefore also the host plant of the caterpillar. Before a caterpillar starts to eat a leaf, it gnaws through the midrib. In this way it prevents the (poisonous) plant sap from being transported into the leaf. It then starts to eat the only slightly poisonous leaf. The caterpillar does not digest the poison, but stores it in its bodily tissues. This makes it inedible to birds. Its bright yellow and black markings are a warning against the poison in its body. Monarch caterpillars grow very quickly and pupate within two weeks. The butterfly which emerges from the pupa still has the poison in its body. Because of this, Monarchs have a distinctive orange and black coloration to frighten off predators. In

Danau plexippus, *Monarch*

the United States of America, this first generation migrates further north. There is still time for a few more generations before autumn, by which time they have reached Canada. Butterflies that emerge from the autumn brood, behave very differently. They do not reproduce, but are mainly busy building up a large fat reserve. They do this until it is time for the trek of more than 3,000 kilometres down to Mexico, where they hibernate in exactly the same forests as the previous winter brood.

Danaus gilippus

Danaus gilippus

Danaus gilippus can be found in the southern parts of the U.S.A,, Cuba, Jamaica and in Central America as far south as Panama. It is regularly spotted in the company of *D. plexippus*, but is itself not a migratory butterfly. The butterfly likes to visit the flowers of the milkweed plant *Asclepias* and those of *Lippia*. The eggs are mainly laid on *Asclepias*, but also on other plants such as *Nerium oleander* and *Sarcostemma*. Some butterflies, which when they were caterpillars did not eat poisonous plants, are left alone by predators because they are indistinguishable from the poisonous butterflies of the species. The brownish orange colours with the distinctive black markings are imitated by butterflies from other families.

Euploea core

Euploea core

Euploea core can be found from India, throughout Southeast Asia to New Guinea and Australia. The butterfly can be found in the gardens of villages and cities, searching for flowers to visit. The main host plant of the caterpillar is oleander (Apocynaceae). This plants contain certain substances which are poisonous to vertebrates, such as birds. The caterpillar stores this poison in its body and is transferred to the butterfly. The poisonous butterfly is a model immitated by many edible butterfly species, such as the female of *Hypolimnas bolina*.

Euploea leucostictos

Euploea leucostictos

Euploea leucostictos has a distribution area which stretches from Burma, Thailand and Malaysia up to New Guinea, the Solomon Islands and the Fiji Islands. The

Euploea leucostictos

Euploea leucostictos

wingspan varies between 6 and 8.5 centimetres. The colours on the wings of this butterfly vary a lot. The caterpillars eat the leaves of *Fiscus wassa, Fiscus subulata* and *Fiscus robusta* (Moraceae). These plants are not poisonous and so, unlike the other *Euploea* species, *Euploea leucostictos* is probably not poisonous either. Therefore butterflies belonging to other families do not imitate this *Euploea* species. But in point of fact, *Euploea leucostictos* imitates poisonous butterflies in its own distribution area, which is usually another *Euploea* species. As a consequence there are many different forms within this species.

Euploea mulciber

Euploea mulciber can be found from India and southern China to Indonesia. It is a typical inhabitant of forests and flies in open spaces and along the edges of the forest. The males of this butterfly species have a blue sheen on the upper side of their wings, visible when the sun falls on

Euploea mulciber

them from the right angle. The host plants of *Euploea mulciber* are oleander (Apocynaceae) and many species of aristolochias (Aristolochiaceae). Since these plants are poisonous, the butterfly is also poisonous. The colours and markings on its wings are imitated by other butterflies.

Idea blanchardi

Idea blanchardi

Idea blanchardi can only be found on the Indonesian island of Sulawesi. Nevertheless, various subspecies are known. This is because most of the *Idea* species vary in their coloration. The caterpillar's host plants are tylophora and parsonis. Because of its large wingspan, the flight of *Idea blanchardi* is slow and gliding.

Idea idea

Idea idea

Idea idea can only be found on some of the Molucca islands. It is an inhabitant of dense rain forests and usually flies just below the treetops. It is quite a large butterfly with a wingspan of 12 to 14 centimetres. The body of an *Idea* is only small and so it does not have many muscles. This is why *Idea* butterflies are not very strong flyers. They beat their wings a couple of times every now and again, but most of the time they glide. *Idea idea* is characterised by the small amount of dark markings on the wings.

Idea leuconoe

Idea leuconoe

Idea leuconoe occurs in a very specific area. It can be found from southern China and Malaysia to the Philippines and a few Indonesian islands. The butterfly inhabits dense rain forests. The host plant of the caterpillars is tylophora. *Idea leuconoe* is an especially large butterfly. The wingspan is usually larger than 15 centimetres. Its wingbeat is slow and distinctive due to the large size of its wings. The butterfly does not get eaten by birds because it contains strong poisons such as alkaloids.

Idea lynceus

Idea lynceus has a distribution area which stretches from Sri Lanka and

Idea lynceus

India through Indo-China to Malaysia and some of the Indonesian islands. With its wingspan of 16.5 centimetres, it is the largest representative of the genus. It prefers to fly in very wooded areas. Males and females are identical in their coloration and patterns of markings. The amount and size of the markings can vary in each region.

Lycorea cleobaea

Lycorea cleobaea is an American butterfly found from Mexico to Peru. Its fore-wings are long and narrow for a butterfly belonging to the Danaidae family. The reason for this is mimicry. A *Lycorea* looks exactly like a *Mechanitis* or *Heliconius*. These are butterfly genera which have long, narrow fore-wings and warning colours. The caterpillars of *Lycorea cleobaea* live on *Carica papaya* (Caricaceae), *Fiscus* (Moraceae) and *Asclepias curassavica* (Asclepiadaceae).

Lycorea cleobea

pias curassavica (Asclepiadaceae). Immature caterpillars gnaw out a piece of leaf and only eat it after an hour. Older caterpillars gnaw through the midrib of a leaf before eating it. By doing this, the caterpillars prevent too many poisonous substances from getting into their food. The plants try to defend themselves against being eaten by making distasteful chemical substances in their leaves. This makes the leaves inedible. By gnawing through the leaf veins at the right place, the caterpillar prevents the leaf from being inedible. The butterflies fly in densely wooded areas. Males occupy a sunny spot in the forest and chase away all other butterflies with the same colouring. Females spend the afternoon laying eggs. They sometimes leave the woods to lay eggs in open areas.

Parantica cleona

Parantica cleona

Parantica cleona (formerly *Danaus cleona*) can be found on Sulawesi in Indonesia. Unlike many *Paranticas*, the base colour on the wings is not white, but yellowish orange. The veins on the wings have the wide dark edges which are characteristic of the Danaidae. The butterflies of this family have warning colours. They are also quite resistant to attack by birds. If a bird pecks one of these distasteful butterflies, it does not do much damage, but finds out that it had better not eat this butterfly. The arrangement of strong scales on the butterfly's body is what makes this species so tough.

Parantica schenkii

Parantica schenkii (formerly *Danaus schenkii*) can be found from New Guinea to the Solomon Islands. With its wingspan of less than 6.5 centimetres it is one of the smallest members of the Danaidae family. The dorsal and ventral surfaces of the butterfly are identical. There are also no differences in appearance between the males and females. They fly in secluded woods and in places where the rain forest has recovered from the chopping down of trees. This is where they can find their host plants. Females lay their eggs on the tendrils of *Asclepias* plants.

Parantica weiskei

Parantica weiskei

The distribution area of *Parantica weiskei* (formerly *Danaus weiskei*) is restricted to New Guinea. It is a rare butterfly, which lives in mountainous areas at a height of 1,500 to 2,000 metres. Out of almost 20 species of the Danaidae family found on New Guinea, this species lives at the highest altitudes. The wingspan of the females is 7 centimetres, and that of the males is only 6 centimetres. Males can be recognised by the distinctive circular black markings on the outer margin of the hind-wings.

Parantica schenkii

Riodinidae

Hamearis lucina, *Duke of Burgundy Fritillary*

Hamearis lucina

Hamearis lucina

Hamearis lucina, the Duke of Burgundy Fritillary (Riodinidae family), flies in the shelter of the edges of wooded areas in a large part of Europe. This butterfly is similar in appearance to a Fritillary, but its behaviour is more like a Blue. This is why *Hamaearis lucina* has been put into a separate family. The butterflies fly in May and June. Sometimes there is a small second generation in the southern part of Europe. The butterfly lays its eggs on various species of primulas (Primulaceae). The caterpillars grow quickly and generally pupate within a month. The pupa hibernates hidden in between the leaf litter.

Taenaris catops

Taenaris catops (Amathusiidae family) is a characteristic representative of a genus with a large number of species found on New Guinea and the surrounding islands. The butterfly is found in a large number of various areas, from open terrains to dense rain forest and from sea level to a height of 1,500 metres. Sometimes it flies long distances over open terrain, but it prefers to stay in the shady areas in the forest. Both males and females of *Taenaris catops* drink the juices of rotting fruit. They also drink the sap of the palm-like cycads (sago palms), which they find on cut off leaf stalks or in the rotting seed pods which have fallen from the trees. The sap of these cycads contains a poisonous substance, cycasine. Because of this, the butterfly is inedible to insect eaters. Many other butterflies imitate the appearance of *Taenaris* so as to seem inedible themselves. The host plants of the caterpillar are *Cordyline terminalis* (Liliaceae), musa (Musaceae), *Areca catechu* and *Caryota rumphiana* (Arecaceae). The butterfly has a wingspan of 7.5 to 9.5 centimetres. In general, the females are larger than the males. The distinctive eyespots on the underside of the wings are only slightly visible on the upper surface.

Taenaris catops, *dorsal surface*

Taenaris catops, *ventral surface*

14 Moths

Brahmaea wallichii

Brahmaea wallichii

Brahmaea wallichii can be found in the northern part of India, in Burma, China and Japan. This butterfly, which can have a wingspan of 16 centimetres, is one of the largest representatives of a small butterfly family, the Brahmaeidae. About twenty species belong to this family. The caterpillars live on the leaves of trees such as ash (*Fraxinus*), but in captivity also on the leaves of *Ligustrum* and *Syringa*. The caterpillars are white and yellow with a pattern of black spots. The long, thin, horn-like spines on their head and abdomen are distinctive. They lose these 'horns' when they moult for the last time. The caterpillar stops eating when it is fully grown. It starts to change colour and leaves the host plant to search for a suitable place to pupate. It makes a large hole under the ground and pupates there. In those areas where the butterfly hibernates, this occurs as a pupa under the ground.

Sphingidae - Hawk Moths

The Sphingidae are a family of moths which are found all over the world. Nearly 1,000 species of this family are known, most of which live in the tropical regions. In general, they are large butterflies. The exceptionally large South American *Cocytius antaeus*, for example, has a wingspan of 17.5 centimetres. The Hawk Moths have a distinctively large body.

They are able to fly exceptionally fast due to the long, narrow fore-wings.

The fastest flying butterfly recorded, is a Hawk Moth which reached a speed of 53 kilometres an hour. In spite of their large size, Hawk Moths can hardly ever be spotted. The caterpillars, which are also large, are easier to find. These caterpillars have a pointed spine sticking out from the end of the abdomen.

Smerinthus ocellata, *Eyed Hawk Moth*

Caterpillar of Hyloicus pinastri

Caterpillar of Acherontia atropos, *yellow form*

Caterpillar of Acherontia atropos, *brown form*

Acherontia atropos

Acherontia atropos, Death's Head Hawk Moth, lives in Africa and the southwestern part of Asia. The butterfly migrates from the Mediterranean region northwards into Europe. The migrating butterflies fly in July and August. A second generation, descendants of the migrants, fly from the beginning of September. The caterpillar's host plant is the potato plant, but other species of the nightshade family (Solanaceae) are also eaten. The caterpil-

Caterpillar of Acherontia atropos, *Death's Head Hawk*

lar pupates in a hole under the ground. The proboscis of the Death's Head Hawk Moth is short and strong. It can drink nectar, but also uses the proboscis to pierce honeycombs in beehives and suck up the honey. When disturbed the butterflies sometimes make shrill chirping sounds to confuse their predators.

Agrius cingulata, *Pink-spotted Hawk Moth*

Agrius cingulata

Agrius cingulata, Pink-spotted Hawk Moth, can be found in the southern part of the United States of America, Central America, South America and on Hawaii. In the USA, the large caterpillar of this Hawk Moth can be a serious pest on fields of *Ipomoea*, the sweet potato. For this reason the caterpillar of this butterfly, called the sweet potato hornworm, is controlled in every way possible. The butterfly can easily be recognised by the red-coloured diagonal bands on the body. This coloration does, however, vary between pale pink and bright red throughout the different parts of the distribution area.

Agrius convolvuli

Agrius convolvuli, Convolvulus Hawk Moth, has a distribution area stretching from Africa, Europe and Asia up to Australia. The butterflies which fly in Europe have emerged from the pupa in Africa and flown northwards. The pupa hibernates. Because the pupa cannot stand

Agrius convolvuli, *Convolvulus Hawk Moth*

frost very well, only the pupae which hibernate in the warmer regions survive. The butterflies, which fly during the evening, like to visit honeysuckle flowers (*Lonicera*) which give off a strong scent to attract pollinating insects at dusk. The caterpillars of *Argrius concolvuli* live on lesser bindweed (*Convolvulus arvensis*).

Cocytius antaeus

Cocytius antaeus

Cocytius antaeus can be found in the tropical parts of South and Central America and in Florida in the United States of America. With its wingspan of 17.5 centimetres, it is the largest species of the Hawk Moth family. Additional distinctive features are the yellow markings on both sides of the body and the yellow base of the hind-wing. There are also large transparent windows on the hindwings. The butterflies are active throughout the year and do not hibernate. The caterpillars eat the leaves of annona.

Coequosa triangularis

Coequosa triangularis

Coequosa triangularis can only be found in the eastern part of Australia. This Hawk Moth can be easily recognised by the dark-coloured triangular markings on its fore-wings. The wingspan of this species can be as large as 16 centimetres. The host plants of the caterpillars include banksia, grevillea, macadamia and other plants in the Proteaceae family. The green caterpillars are covered in yellow and white spines and the back legs have a marking which resembles the eye of a reptile to frighten off predators.

Daphnis nerii, *Oleander Hawk Moth*

Daphnis nerii

Daphnis nerii, Oleander Hawk Moth, can be found throughout most of Africa and in Southeast Asia. The butterfly is active throughout the year in these tropical regions. This large beautiful green and pink-coloured Hawk Moth can sometimes be found in Europe. The wingspan varies between 8 and 12 centimetres. The large caterpillars feed on the periwinkle (*Vinca*) and the oleander (*Nerium*). The latter plant contains a substance called nereine which is very poisonous to vertebrates. The caterpillars are not affected by this poison, but they do not store it in their body either. The caterpillars and butterflies of *Daphnis nerii* do not get any protection from the poison in their host plant, as is the case in many other butterfly species.

Deilephila elpenor

Deilephila elpenor, Elephant Hawk Moth, in common in a large part of Europe and Asia. The host plant is willow-herb, but also many species of bedstraw (*Galium*) get eaten by the caterpillars. Brown and yellow forms of these Hawk Moth caterpillars are found. The

Caterpillar of Deilephila elpenor

Deilephila elpenor, *Elephant Hawk Moth*

Hemaris fuciformis, *Broad-bordered Bee Hawk moth*

front part of the breastplate of the caterpillar is pointed and looks like a sort of trunk. This is where the butterfly gets its name from. They fly at dusk and like to visit honeysuckle flowers. They usually lay their eggs on fuchsia plants in gardens.

Euchloron megaera

Euchloron megaera

Euchloron megaera is widespread in the part of Africa south of the Sahara. It is the only species of the *Euchloron* genus. The butterfly stands out immediately because of the bright-green colour of its body and fore-wings. The colour of the hind-wings varies from yellow to orange. The wingspan varies between 7 and 12 centimetres. The caterpillar's host plants are grapevine (*Vitis vinifera*) and parthenocissus. The caterpillars have large eye-spots on the front of the first segments to frighten off small insect-eating birds.

Hemaris fuciformis

Hemaris fuciformis, Broad-bordered Bee Hawk Moth, can be found in a large part of Europe. It flies in open spaces in woods and near the edges of woods. This Hawk Moth lays its eggs on honeysuckle (*Lonicera*) and snowberry (*Symphoricarpus*). When the caterpillars are fully grown, they pupate in a loosely spun cocoon under the leaf litter. The Broad-bordered Bee Hawk Moth hibernates as a pupa. When it emerges from the pupa, its wings are covered in scales. The butterfly loses most of these scales during its first flight. This results in transparent wings with scales along only the outer margins of the wings. The butterfly mainly flies during the day and searches for flowers on rhododendron and butterfly bushes.

Hyles galii, *Bedstraw Hawk Moth*

Hyles galii

Hyles galii, Bedstraw Hawk Moth, can be found in North America and in

Europe. The butterfly sometimes migrates over long distances. It can mainly be found in dry areas, where the host plants of the caterpillar grow. These host plants are various species of bedstraw (*Gali-um*). The caterpillars spin a cocoon in the leaf litter where they hibernate. There are one to two broods a year. The butter-flies fly during the day and at dusk. They search for flowers to drink nectar from and for butterflies of its own species to mate with.

Laothoe populi

Laothoe populi, Poplar Hawk Moth, has a distribution area which stretches from Western Europe to far east in the temperate regions of Asia. The butterfly, which has two generations a year, can mainly be found near the edges of woods and in parks. The eggs are laid on various species of poplar and willow tree. The caterpillars which hatch out of the eggs are a green to bluish-green colour covered in lots of white and yellow dots. When the caterpillar is fully grown, it pupates in a hole under the ground, where it hibernates. It flies around at night and rests on a tree trunk during the day. It is almost invisible because of its shape and colour.

Manduca sexta

The distribution area of *Manduca sexta*, Carolina Sphinx, stretches from the tropical part of South America to the northern part of the United States of America. The butterfly can be easily recognised by the six pairs of square yellow markings

Laothoe populi, *Poplar Hawk Moth*

Manduca sexta

on the abdomen. The host plants of this Hawk Moth are commercially grown crops belonging to the Solanaceae family, such as tobacco (*Nicotiana*), potato (*Solanum*) and tomato (*Lycopersicum*) in particular. *Manduca sexta* together with *Manduca quinquemaculata* can cause great damage to these crops. They are a very serious pest forming large plagues of insects which cause a lot of damage to the cultivation of tomatoes in America. A successful way of combating this Hawk Moth is by placing traps with virgin females as bait. The mature males are irresistibly attracted by the female's sex pheromones and get caught in a electric trap and are therefore prevented from reproducing.

Protambulix strigilis

Protambulix strigilis

Protambulix strigilis can be found in the tropical regions of Central and South America. The long, narrow fore-wings, which have a dark stripe along the outer margin, are characteristic of this species of Hawk Moth. The wingspan varies between 9.5 and 12 centimetres. The caterpillars are green with diagonal yellow stripes across the body. Their host plant is *Anacardium spondias*. Other plants of the Anacardiaceae family are also eaten.

Pseudosphinx tetrio

Pseudosphinx tetrio

Pseudosphinx tetrio can be found from Paraguay in South America to the Caribbean area and the south of the U.S.A.. The wingspan is 13 to 16 centimetres. When this Hawk Moth keeps still during the day, the grey and brown coloration on the wings and body make sure that it cannot be seen by predators. The host plants of the large caterpillars are jasmine (*Jasminum*) and plumeria.

Smerinthus ocellata

Smerinthus ocellata, Eyed Hawk Moth, can be found throughout Europe. The butterfly lives in woodlands, parks and orchards, where the trees grow which are the caterpillar's host plants. Special favourites are willow, poplar and apple. The caterpillar pupates in a hole under the ground. When an Eyed Hawk Moth sits still, it is extremely well camouflaged. However, if it is disturbed, the butterfly holds up its fore-wings. By doing this the

Smerinthus ocellata, *Eyed Hawk Moth*

distinctive eye-spots on the upper surface of its hind-wings are displayed. This has been proved in experiments to frighten off predators.

Xanthopan morgani

Xanthopan morgani

Xanthopan morgani can be found on Madagascar and in a few tropical areas of Africa. The butterfly, with a wingspan of 10 to 13 centimetres, can be recognised by the dark marking divided in two on the hind-wings. This butterfly has a proboscis which can be as long as 25 centimetres. It uses this extraordinarily long proboscis to drink nectar from the long and very deep flowers of the orchid, *Angraecum sesquipedale*. When Charles Darwin discovered this orchid, he predicted that an insect must exist with a very long proboscis to pollinate the flower. Some years later when this insect, a subspecies of this Hawk Moth,

was discovered, it got given the name *Xanthopan praedicta* (praedicta means the predicted). The caterpillars of this large Hawk Moth live on annona and uvaria plants.

Saturniidae - Emperor Moths

The butterflies belonging to the family of Emperor Moths are found throughout the world. More than 1,000 species are known. Some of the tropical Emperor Moths belong to the largest butterflies in the world. The Giant Atlas Moth (*Attacus atlas imperator*) may have a wingspan of 32 centimetres. Many Emperor Moths have eye-spots and transparent windows in the wings to confuse predators. The proboscis of the butterflies in the Emperor Moth family is either not developed at all or is only partially developed. This is why these butterflies are not able to drink and so they do not live very long. Four or five days is quite long for these moths. The spring-like forked antennae of the members of this family are very sensitive. Male Emperor Moths can usually smell females of its own species miles away. Just before they pupate, the caterpillars spin a strong cocoon of silk thread. They pupate inside this. The cocoons of various species of Emperor Moth are used to make natural silk.

Attacus atlas

Emperor Moth

Actias luna

Actias luna, Luna Moth, can be found in the United States of America and Mexico. The butterfly gets its name from the half moon-shaped markings on the pale green wings. This colour varies from yellow to blue in this species. The butterflies fly in the evening and at night in wooded areas. The females lay their eggs on the leaves of many species of trees, such as birch (*Betula*), alder (*Alnus*), chestnut and willow (*Salix*).

Actias luna, *Luna Moth*

Antherea mylitta

Actias selene, *Indian Luna Moth*

Caterpillar of Actias selene

Actias selene

Actias selene, Indian Luna Moth, can be found from India to China and Indonesia. The wingspan of these moths can reach as much as 12 centimetres. Their long tails usually break off after the first flight. Luna moths have a nervous, dancing way of flying. They are not very particular in the choice of their host plants. They lay their eggs on various trees and bushes, such as Rhododendron. The fat green caterpillars have lines of hairy red warts. Before they pupate, they spin a cocoon on a leaf of the host plant.

Aglia tau, *Tau Emperor*

Aglia tau

Aglia tau, Tau Emperor, has a distribution area which stretches from Europe to Japan in eastern Asia. The butterfly gets its name from the white wing markings which are shaped like the Greek letter t (tau). The butterflies fly in April and May, preferably in deciduous forests. There is one generation a year. The males fly during the day. They are lured by the female Tau Emperors by sexual scents. After mating, the female lays her eggs on the trunks of beech and sometimes also birch trees. The caterpillars crawl up the branches to the buds which come out in the spring and feed on the fresh, young leaves. When they are fully grown, the caterpillars leave the tree to pupate in a hole under the ground, where it hibernates.

Antherea pernyi

Antherea pernyi

Antherea pernyi, Chinese Silkmoth, can be found in China, southeast Russia and Japan. The butterflies lay their eggs on oak trees (*Quercus*). They lay up to 150 eggs in two to three days. Before pupating, the caterpillars spin a cocoon from a long, even silk thread. The cocoons of *Antherea pernyi* are also used commercially to make natural silk, the so-called shantung silk. There are two broods of this Silkmoth a year.

Antherea polyphemus

Antherea polyphemus can be found in the southern part of Canada and in the United States of America. It is the only representative of its genus in the New World and also the most common of the

Antherea polyphemus

Argema mittrei, *male*

Antherea polyphemus

long tails can reach a length of 20 centimetres. Males not only have much wider antennae, but also much longer tails on their hind-wings. These tails usually break off after a few flights. The host plant of the caterpillars of the Malagasy Luna Moth is eugenia.

The caterpillars make pure white-coloured cocoons with a distinctive holey structure. This butterfly is an

Argema mittrei

Emperor Moths in North America. In the northern part of the distribution area, there is one generation a year, in the southern, warmer regions there are two generations a year.

The butterfly is not particular in the choice of its host plant, more than 50 tree and bush species are known on which the female lays her eggs. Apple (*Malus*) and hawthorn (*Crataegus*) are two of the examples on their menu. Males and females have the same colours. The coloration of this Emperor Moth varies a lot within its distribution area. The base colour can vary from yellow to reddish brown.

Argema mittrei

Argema mittrei, Malagasy Luna Moth, can only be found on Madagascar. The butterflies have a wingspan of 18 centimetres, whereas their exceptionally

endangered species in the wild, but is bred successfully in so-called butterfly farms on Madagascar.

Attacus atlas, *Asian Atlas Moth*

Caterpillar of Attacus atlas

Attacus atlas

Attacus atlas, Asiatic Atlas Moth, has a particularly large distribution area. It stretches from India, Indonesia and Malaysia to China. Many subspecies of this large moth are known. The wing surface area of the Giant Atlas Moth (Attacus atlas imperator) is not exceeded by any other butterfly species. Atlas Moths have a very distinctive marking resembling a snake's head on the end of their fore-wing. This keeps their enemies away. The caterpillars feed on the leaves of a wide range of tree species. The very large caterpillars have fleshy outgrowths along their body and are covered in a whitish powder. They camouflage their cocoons wonderfully by spinning them onto a leaf.

Automeris io

Automeris io

Automeris io is a North American Emperor Moth, which lives from Mexico to the southern part of Canada. The butterfly is not at all particular in the choice of its host plant. Nearly everything that is green seems to be eaten. However, when the caterpillars have eaten a certain species of plant, they do not change over to another plant. Then they have become very particular. The caterpillars, when still small, live together in large numbers. After they have shed their skin three times, they go off on their own. They pupate in a thin cocoon, which they sometimes spin in between the leaves of the host plant and sometimes under the ground. The pupa hibernates in the cocoon. The wingspan of *Automeris io* is 8 centimetres. When resting, the butterfly folds its fore-wings over the top of its hind-wings. When disturbed, it lifts up its fore-wings and by doing this, suddenly uncovers a pair of large eyes so as to frighten off its enemies.

Callosamia promethea

Callosamia promethea is an Emperor Moth which lives in North America. It can be found from the southern part of Canada to the southeast of the United States of America. The butterfly has a wingspan of 8 to 10 centimetres. Females of this species are reddish brown with characteristic red markings along the edges of the wings. The females are active

is one of the largest butterflies in the world. It can be found on Papua New Guinea and in the northern part of Australia. Female Hercules Silkmoths have especially wide wings, whereas the males stand out because of the extremely long tails on their hind-wings. The butterflies fly at night. The caterpillar's host plants are *Homolanthus* and *Dysoxylum*. Not only are the butterflies very large, but the caterpillars can also reach enormous sizes. Hercules Silkmoth caterpillars 17 centimetres long are no exception.

at night. The males of *Callosamia promethea* on the other hand fly during the day. They are much darker coloured, sometimes even black, and, especially when flying, look like *Battus philenor*, a poisonous member of the Orniothoptera from the same region. The butterflies lay their eggs on a large range of trees and bushes.

Coscinocera hercules

Coscinocera hercules, Hercules Silkmoth, gets its name from the fact that it

Dictyoploca simla

Dictyoploca simla, formerly also called *Saturnia simla*, can be found in Asia. The host plants of the caterpillar of this Emperor Moth are species of prunus. The butterflies lay neat rows of eggs on the branches of the host plant. The egg is the stage of this butterfly's life cycle in which they pass the winter. When the leaves start to grow on the trees, the caterpillars start to hatch out of the eggs.

Coscinocera hercules

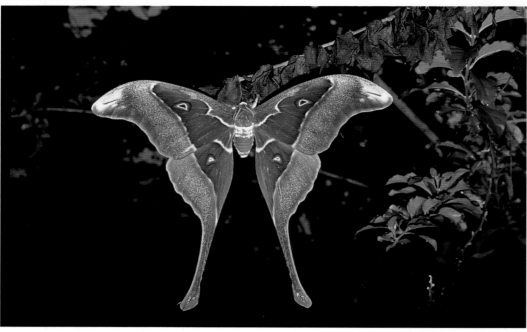

Dictyoploca simla

(*Malus*) and willow (*Salix*). When the caterpillar is fully grown, it pupates in an untidy cocoon where it hibernates. *Hyalophora cecropia* is one of the few Emperor Moths which does not have windows in its wings. The colour of the butterfly depends on the temperature at which it spent the pupal stage. The hotter the temperature at the pupal stage, the brighter the red colour of the butterfly.

They are colourful caterpillars with a wonderful head of blue hair. When the caterpillar is fully grown, it spins a cocoon with a loose, open structure in which it pupates. The chrysalis is not hidden but is clearly visible. It seems vulnerable, but the cocoon is strong enough to provide good protection against attack by predators. The butterflies have a wingspan of 12 to 15 centimetres. *Dictyoploca simla* flies in September and October.

Rothschildia jacobaea

Rothschildia jacobaea

Rothschildia jacobaea is a large American Emperor Moth. The wingspan can be as much as 15 centimetres. It gets its name from Walter Rothschild, the founder of one of the largest butterfly collections in the world. This collection can be seen in the British Museum. There are about 30 species of butterflies in the *Rothschildia* genus, most of which live in South America and Central America. The large transparent windows in the wings are characteristic of this Emperor Moth. The butterflies are in a manner of speaking the American equivalent of the Giant Atlas Moths of Asia.

Hyalophora cecropia

Hyalophora cecropia

Hyalophora cecropia is the most well-known representative of the four species of the genus *Hyalophora*, which is only found in North America. The butterfly can be seen from March to June in the southern part of Canada and in the United States of America. Further south, it gets more and more rare. The female lays her eggs on the leaves of broad-leaved trees such as maple (*Acer*), prunus, apple

Samia cynthia

Samia cynthia, Ailanthus Silkmoth, originally comes from Asia. It was originally introduced into North America and Europe to make silk, but where it survives very well. Its host plant is not restricted to the tree of heaven (*Ailanthus*), since

Saturnia pavonia

Samia cynthia, *Ailanthus Silkmoth*

Caterpillar of Saturnia pavonia

privet, lilac and other plants are also acceptable to the caterpillars. The caterpillars of the Ailanthus Silkmoth are covered in a whitish powder at later stages of development and grow very quickly. Before they pupate, they spin a cocoon in which they also hibernate.

Saturnia pavonia

Saturnia pavonia, Emperor Moth, can be found in a large part of Europe and Asia. The butterflies have a preference for heathlands and high moorlands, but also fly in rocky steppes and in deciduous forests. The butterflies are not very particular about what they eat because they feed on a large variety of plants, such as heather, blackberry and cinquefoil. There is one generation a year. The Emperor Moth hibernates as a pupa, safely in a cocoon. It is known that the Giant Peacock Moth (*Saturnia pyri*) sometimes hibernates for three winters in the pupal stage. The female of the Giant Peacock Moth is the largest butterfly in Europe.

Saturnia pavoria, *Emperor Moth*

Lythria cruentaria

Geometridae - Geometrid Moths

Perconia strigillaria

The Geometridae family has a large number of species which are found throughout the world. More than 15,000 different species are known. It is the second largest butterfly family. The butterflies are usually fragile and small with a slim body. The females of some species are wingless. Therefore they cannot fly.

Rheumaptera undulata

The Geometrids get their family name from the characteristic way the caterpillars move, these caterpillars are called stick caterpillars or loopers. These caterpillars push both pairs of abdominal prolegs against the front pair of legs. This makes the body into an arch above the legs. It then grips onto the branch with its abdominal prolegs and stretches its body forward in a looping movement. It progresses by moving one length of its body forward at a time and it looks like it is measuring the distance. When the stick caterpillar or looper is resting, it grips onto a branch with only its abdominal pair of prolegs. To be safe, it spins a silken thread onto the branch which it holds on to with its mouth-parts. If the stick caterpillar falls or in emergencies it lets itself drop, it stays attached to the branch by this life line. By using this thread, it can climb back onto the branch.

Abraxas grossulariata

Abraxas grossulariata, Magpie Moth, can be found in Europe and in the temperate regions of Asia. This small, colourful butterfly has a wingspan of 4 centimetres. It flies in June and July. There is one generation a year. This moth is considered to be a pest and so has been controlled for many years because of the damage the caterpillars cause to gooseberry and currant bushes. The sloe and hazel are also eaten by the caterpillars. The Magpie Moth hibernates as a caterpillar

Abraxas grossulariata

on the host plant. The following spring, it eats the buds and young leaves. The caterpillar pupates in a cocoon in a rolled-up leaf. These butterflies fly mainly at night, but are also active during the day.

Abraxas sylvata

Abraxas sylvata, Clouded Magpie, can be found in Europe and in the temperate regions of Asia. It flies in wooded areas. The butterfly lays its eggs on a large variety of tree species, especially elm, beech and bird cherry. The caterpillar of the Clouded Magpie hibernates. In spring, the caterpillar is fully grown and pupates in a cocoon underneath the ground. The butterflies fly from June to October. Usually there is one, but sometimes also a second generation.

Erannis defoliaria

Erannis defoliaria, Mottled Umber, can be found in a large part of Europe. The butterflies are not particular about their

Erannis defoliaria

Catospilos sylvatus

choice of host plant. Nearly every species of tree is to their liking. They sometimes cause a lot of damage in orchards. The flight time of the butterfly is very unusual, because it is in December and January. The females of the Mottled Umber do not have any wings. At night, they crawl up against a tree trunk and wait for the males which fly around at this time. After mating, they lay their eggs on the trees. In spring, the caterpillars feed on the young, tender leaves. Just before the summer, the caterpillars let themselves drop to the ground on a long silken thread and subsequently pupate underneath the ground. This is where the pupae spend the summer. The first frosts of autumn are the sign for the butterflies to emerge from the pupae.

Geometra papilionaria

Geometra papilionaria, Large Emerald, can be found in the temperate and cold areas of Europe and Asia. It flies in wooded areas. There is one generation a

Geometra papilionaria

year. The butterflies fly in the summer. They lay their eggs on a large variety of broad-leaved trees such as oak, birch, elm and hazel. The Large Emerald hibernates as a small caterpillar. The brown caterpillar clasps onto a branch and is almost invisible. When the buds come out and the leaves start to grow on the trees in spring, the caterpillar changes colour. It turns brown with green markings and so is still camouflaged with the change in the season.

Milionia aroensis

Milionia aroensis

Milionia aroensis is a Geometrid Moth which can only be found in New Guinea. More than forty species of the genus *Milionia* are known, most of which can be found in New Guinea and on a few Indonesian islands. Males have a distinctive red band across their fore-wings, females a yellow one. Dorsal and ventral surfaces are almost identical. The wingspan is 4.5 centimetres. The butterflies have a distinctive bright red and pitch black sheen. *Milionia* clearly demonstrates that not all moths are dull coloured.

Ourapteryx sambucaria, *Swallow-tailed Moth*

Ourapteryx sambucaria

Ourapteryx sambucaria, Swallow-tailed Moth, can be found in Europe and in the temperate regions of Asia. The caterpillars feed on many species of trees and bushes, especially on sloe, hawthorn, ivy and privet. The butterflies are mainly active at night. If disturbed during the day, they fly up in the air and look exactly like butterflies. There is one generation a year. The females of the Swallow-tailed Moth lay their eggs together in groups on the leaves of the host plant. The caterpillars start to grow in the autumn and hibernate at the immature stage. In spring, they carry on growing. Before pupating, the caterpillar spins a cocoon on the underside of a leaf. The butterflies fly in July and August.

Selenia dentaria

Selenia dentaria

Selenia dentaria, Early Thorn, can be found in Europe and in the temperate regions of Asia. The butterfly usually flies in woodlands. Their eggs are laid on a large variety of tree species but preferably on hawthorn and sloe. Caterpillars on the host plant, look exactly like twigs and are almost inconspicuous. When the caterpillar is fully grown, it spins a cocoon under the leaf litter, where the Early Thorn hibernates. There are usually two broods a year. The appearance of the second generation differs quite a lot from the moths which fly in April and May. They are much smaller and a lot less brightly coloured.

Timandra griseata

Timandra griseata, Blood-vein Moth, lives in Northern Africa and in Europe. It can be found in verges and near the edges of ditches. This is where the but-

Timandra griseata

terfly searches for various species of sorrel (*Rumex*), the caterpillar's host plant. The flight time is from May to October. There are two broods. Hibernation takes place at the caterpillar stage. That is why the caterpillar of the Blood-vein Moth can be found all year round. Just before pupation, the caterpillar spins a loose cocoon with an open structure. The beautiful green-coloured moth is active at night and rests on tree trunks and leaves during the day.

Cerura vinula

Cerura vinula, Puss Moth, belongs to the Notodontidae family. This species can be found throughout Europe and in Asia as far as Japan. The butterfly can usually be found in woods where low poplars and willows grow. The Puss Moth is a large moth with a wingspan of about 7 centimetres. The adult butterflies do not eat. The caterpillar looks very

Cerura vinula, *Puss Moth*

unusual. It has a prominent red protruberance on its head, which frightens off predators. In addition, it has two appendages at the hind end which can shoot out long red threads. And as if this was not enough, it can also spit formic acid at its enemies. When the caterpillar is fully grown, it spins a hard woody cocoon onto the bark of the tree. This is where the Puss Moth hibernates.

Caterpillar of Phalera bucephala

Phalera bucephala, *Buff-tip Moth*

Phalera bucephala

Phalera bucephala, Buff-tip Moth, belongs to the Notodontidae family. The butterfly can be found throughout Europe and in Asia up to Siberia. The flight time is from May to September. There are usually two generations a year. The host plants of the caterpillars are various species of trees, mainly oaks and willows. The large caterpillars live together in large numbers and strip a branch completely bare of its leaves before starting on a new branch. When the caterpillar is fully grown, it makes a hole under the ground and fills it with a cocoon. This is where the caterpillar pupates. The chrysalis hibernates in this underground hole and sometimes stays there for a second winter. The butterflies have no mouthparts and cannot drink nectar. The Buff-tip Moths fly from May. When the butterflies rest on a branch, they are inconspicuous. Due to the markings and the colours on their head and wings they look exactly like a broken off twig.

Caterpillar of Arctia caja

Arctiidae - Tiger Moths

Arctia caja

Arctia caja, Garden Tiger, is one of the most well-known representatives of the Arctiidae (Tiger Moths), a butterfly family with about 8,000 species. The Garden Tiger can be found in Europe, Asia and

Arctia caja, *Garden Tiger*

North America. Females lay their eggs on various plants, such as low-growing shrubs, stinging nettle, and sorrel. The caterpillars are very hairy. This is where the butterfly gets its name from. The caterpillars hibernate at an early stage. In spring, they pupate in a cocoon, into which the irritating hairs of the caterpillar are spun. The wingspan of the Garden Tiger is 6 to 7 centimetres. In spite of their size, the butterflies are inconspicuous as long as they sit still. When disturbed, they show their bright red hind-wings. By showing such bright colours, in contrast to the mottled pattern of the fore-wings, they frighten most predators away. The butterflies do not have any mouth-parts and so are unable to feed.

Diacrisia sannio, *Clouded Buff*

Diacrisia sannio

Diacrisia sannio, Clouded Buff (Arctiidae family), is found in Europe and in the western part of Asia. It is a Tiger Moth which feels at home in heathlands, where the caterpillar's host plants are found, namely various species of sorrel (*Rumex*) and plantain (*Plantago*). There is one brood of this moth a year. The butterflies fly in June and at the beginning of July. At the end of autumn, the immature caterpillar crawls away and hibernates.
At the end of spring, when the caterpillar is fully grown, it pupates in a cocoon, spun on the ground at the foot of the host plant. Male Clouded Buffs fly dur-

ing the day, whereas the females of the species are active at night.

Euplagia quadripunctaria, *Jersey Tiger*

Euplagia quadripunctaria

Euplagia quadripunctaria, Jersey Tiger (Arctiidae family), can be found from Central Europe up to Central Asia. The butterfly flies during the day and likes sunny places. There is one brood a year. The butterflies fly in July and August. They lay their eggs on a large variety of plants, for example dandelion and plantain. The Jersey Tiger hibernates as a small caterpillar. The chrysalis of the Jersey Tiger is spun in the leaf litter. This Tiger Moth is famous for the huge numbers in which it can be found yearly on the island Rhodos.

Rhyparia purpurata, *Purple Tiger*

Rhyparia purpurata

Rhyparia purpurata, Purple Tiger (Arctiidae family), can be found in the temperate regions of Europe and Asia up to

China. The butterfly likes dry moors and sandy areas. The butterfly lays its eggs on a large variety of low-growing plants and bushes and even trees. The Purple Tiger hibernates as a caterpillar. There is one generation a year. The butterflies are active during the day and fly in June and July.

Spilosoma lubricipeda, *White Ermine*

Spilosoma lubricipeda

Spilosoma lubricipeda, White Ermine (Arctiidae family), has a distribution area which stretches from Northern Africa, through Europe, as far as eastern Asia. The butterfly is a pure white colour with dark dots. The female lays her eggs on a large variety of low-growing herbs and sometimes on trees. It does not have a special preference for a host plant. The immature caterpillar hibernates. In spring, the caterpillar pupates in a cocoon spun onto a leaf of the host plant. There is one generation a year. The White Ermine flies from April to July. The butterfly is inedible to birds.

Cossus cossus

Cossidae

Cossus cossus

Cossus cossus

Cossus cossus, Goat Moth (Cossidae family), is found in North Africa, Europe and Asia. The butterfly is found in wooded areas and orchards. The host plants of the caterpillar are broad-leaved trees, especially various species of willow and poplar. The butterflies lay their eggs in places where the bark of the tree is damaged. The caterpillars live in the trunk and gnaw tunnels in the wood. They grow very slowly. Their whole developmental process can take up to two or three years. When the large pink caterpillars are fully grown, they leave the tree and search for somewhere to pupate. They do this in a cocoon under the ground. The butterflies fly in May, June and July and are active at night. During the day, they rest on a tree trunk and are almost inconspicuous because of their camouflaging colours.

Zeuzera pyrina

Zeuzera pyrina, Leopard moth (Cossidae family), has an particularly extensive distribution area which stretches from Northern Africa, Europe and Asia to North America. The butterflies are not very critical in the choice of their host plant. They lay their eggs on a large variety of broad-leaved trees. The caterpillars live in the trunk and eat the wood. They

Zeuzera pyrina, *Leopard Moth*

grow so slowly, that they usually hibernate twice. When eventually they are fully grown, they pupate in a cocoon which is spun at the end of a tunnel in the tree trunk. They fly throughout the Summer.

Aneda rivularis

Noctuidae - Noctuid Moths

The Nocyuidae or the Noctuid Moth

Xanthia togata

family is the largest family of butterflies. More than 20,000 species of butterflies belong to this family. They are generally uninteresting, dull-coloured butterflies, which are active at night but a few species also fly during the day. *Thysania agrippina* belongs to this family, a South American butterfly which is generally considered to be the largest butterfly in the world. A wingspan of more than 30 centimetres is no exception. The other Noctuid Moths are much smaller in size.

Dichonia aprilina

Catocala fraxini, *Blue Underwing*

Bena prasinana

Catocala fraxini

Catocala fraxini, the Blue Underwing, can be found in an area ranging from North and Central America to the eastern part of Asia. The butterfly lives in woods, where it can find trees such as ash, oak and poplar. The butterfly lays its eggs on these trees. The egg is the stage in which the Blue Underwing overwinters. In the spring, the caterpillars eat and grow until they pupate inside a cocoon which they spin in the leaf litter. The butterflies fly in July and August.

Catocala nupta

Catocala nupta, Red Underwing, can be found in a large part of Europe and Asia. The butterflies fly in woods, parks, wooded banks and gardens, searching for their host plants: willow and poplar. The eggs which the butterfly lays on this plant are also the stage in which the Red Underwing hibernates. When the grey caterpillar is fully grown, it pupates in the leaf lit-

Catocala nupta, *Red Underwing*

Catocala nupta

ter. The moth flies at night. During the day, it sits still and hides its red hind-wings beneath it fore-wings. When disturbed, it suddenly shows the bright red hind-wings to frighten off the predator.

Callistege mi, *Mother Shipton*

Callistege mi

Callistege mi, Mother Shipton, can be found in Europe and Asia. It prefers wet

areas, such as marshes and fields near the edges of wooded areas. The butterfly lays its eggs on various species of clover (*Trifolium*). There is one brood a year. Before it pupates, the caterpillar makes a cocoon in between the grass stalks. The pupa also hibernates. The butterflies fly in May and June. Mother Shiptons fly during the day. The exceptional markings on the upper side of their fore-wings resemble a witch's head.

Phlogophora meticulosa, *Angle Shades*

Phlogophora meticulosa

Phlogophora meticulosa, Angle Shades, has a distribution area which stretches from Northern Africa through Europe to the western part of Asia. The butterfly is not particular at all about the choice of host plant, a large variety of herbs and shrubs qualify. Because of this, the caterpillars can sometimes cause considerable damage in gardens. It pupates in a cocoon spun underneath the ground. The Angle Shades do not hibernate at a specific stage. Both the caterpillar and the pupa can hibernate. The butterflies are active at night and visit flowers to feed on the nectar.

Polychrysia moneta

Polychrysia moneta, Golden Plusia, can be found in Europe and Asia in regions with a temperate climate. Its finds its

Polychrisia moneta, *Golden Plusia*

host plants in parks and public gardens: delphinium (*Delphinium*) and monkshood (*Aconitum*). The Golden Plusia hibernates as an immature caterpillar. Fully grown caterpillars pupate in a cocoon on the host plant. There are two broods a year. The butterflies fly from June up to September. The Golden Plusia is active at night and visits flowers for nectar.

Thysania agrippina

Thysania agrippina

Thysania agrippina has a distribution area which stretches from Central America to the southern part of Brazil in South America. It is a very spectacular representative of the Noctuid Moths, because it is the largest butterfly in the world. The Giant Atlas Moth (*Attacus atlas imperator*) and *Ornithoptera alexandrae* are also mentioned here in this context. The wingspan of *Thysania agrippina* may be more than 30 centimetres. Other butter-

flies of the genus *Thysania* look very much like this species, but are smaller versions of their large relative. The host plants of the caterpillars of this giant Noctuid Moth are plants belonging to the Leguminosae family.

Lasiocampidae – Eggars and Lappet Moths

Gastropacha quercifolia, *Lappet*

Gastropacha quercifolia

Gastropacha quercifolia, Lappet (Lasiocamidae family), is a bombycid which is found throughout Europe and Asia. It prefers to fly in woods, orchards and marshlands, where trees such as sloe (*Prunus spinosa*) and willow (Sailicaceae) grow. The butterfly lays its eggs on these trees. The immature Lappet caterpillar hibernates. When the butterfly sits still, it resembles a bunch of dry oak leaves.

Lasiocampa quercus

Lasiocampa quercus, Oak Eggar (Lasiocampidae family), is a bombycid which flies in Northern Africa and in Europe. The butterfly flies in July and August. The butterfly lays its eggs on a large variety of plants: on trees such as hawthorn (*Crataegus*) and willow (*Calluna*). The immature caterpillar hibernates. In the following spring, the caterpillar grows and pupates quickly. If growth is not so fast, the Oak Eggar hibernates for a second

Lasiocampa quercus, *Oak Eggar*

Calliteara pudibunda

Calliteara pudibunda, *Pale Tussock*

time. This time the pupa is in a cocoon, which is spun in the leaf litter, waiting for the following summer. The females of the Oak Eggar only fly at night time, but the males also fly during the day.

Lymantriidae –
Tussock Moths

Calliteara pudibunda

Calliteara pudibunda, Pale Tussock (Lymantriidae family), can be found in a large part of Europe and Asia, especially in wooded areas. This butterfly lays its eggs on oaks (*Quercus* sp.) and other broad-leaved trees. The yellow, hairy caterpillars are covered with lots of white hairy tufts. The caterpillars feed on the leaves of the trees until they are fully grown. They then crawl into cracks in the bark of the tree trunk where they spin a

cocoon and pupate. This is where they also hibernate. The butterflies fly in May.

Euproctis similis

Euproctis similis, Yellow Tail (Lymantriidae family), can be found throughout Europe and Asia, especially in wooded areas and parks. The butterflies, which fly in July, lay groups of eggs on hawthorn

Euproctis similis, *donsvlinder*

(*Crataegus* sp.) and sloe (*Prunus* sp.). The caterpillars feed on the leaves until winter. Then they each spin a separate cocoon, in which they hibernate. In the spring, Yellow Tail caterpillars carry on growing until they pupate in a cocoon which they spin on the host plant.

Thyatiridae

Habrosyne pyritoides

Habrosyne pyritoides

Habrosyne pyritoides (Thyatiridae family), can be found in Europe and Asia. It lives in wooded areas, where it searches for blackberry bushes which is the plant on which it lays its eggs. There is one brood a year. The pupa hibernates in a cocoon, which lies hidden in the leaf litter. The butterflies fly in June and July. A feature of the genus *Habrosyne* is the loop-shaped marking on the fore-wings.

Uraniidae - Uraniid Moths

Alcides aurora

Alcides aurora

Alcides aurora can be found on New Guinea and on a few other islands in the Bismarck Archipelago. It is one of the eleven *Alcides* species which live in Australia. The butterflies can be compared to their relatives in the tropical parts of America, the Uraniids, and to the Chrysiridias, which live in Africa. They are moths which behave like butterflies in every way. They fly during the day and the way they fly is very similar to that of a butterfly. Not only do they have the beautiful colouring of butterflies, but they also have the lovely green and pale pink sheen, which shines in the sunlight. *Alcides aurora* has a wingspan of 8 centimetres.

Alcides zodiaca

Alcides zodiaca

Alcides zodiaca can be found on New Guinea and in the northern part of Australia. The butterfly has a beautiful pink sheen on its body and wings. The strongly lobed hind-wings with tiny tails are very characteristic. The wingspan is 8.5 to 10 centimetres. Like butterflies, these moths also visit flowers during the day to drink nectar and fly around the treetops at dusk. The caterpillars host plants include plants of the genus *Omphalea* (Euphorbiaceae). This plant is poisonous and it seems likely that the brightly-coloured butterflies are as well.

Chrysiridia riphaeus

Chrysiridia riphaeus can only be found on Madagascar. This beautifully-coloured moth has a wingspan of more than 10 centimetres. The butterfly flies

Chrysiridia riphaeus

during the day and prefers to visit flowers. It can be seen throughout the year, but flies in large numbers only from May to July. The host plant is *Omphalea*, a poisonous plant in the Euphorbiaceae family. *Chrysiridia croesus*, which looks very much like *Chrysiridia riphaeus*, can be found in the eastern part of Africa. Both species are the only representatives of the genus *Chrysiridia*.

Chrysiridia riphaeus

Lyssa patroclus

Lyssa patroclus

Lyssa patroclus, formerly called *Nyctalemon patroclus*, can be found from India and China, throughout the whole of Southeast Asia to the northern part of Australia. *Lyssa* is a genus of about ten butterfly species, which unlike the rest of this family behave like moths. In the evening and at night time, they visit flowers to drink nectar and during the day they hide. They are inconspicuous then because they do not have distinctive iridescent colours.

Urania sloanus

Urania sloanus

The distribution area of *Urania sloanus* is restricted to Jamaica. Seven other *Urania* species, of which *Urania leilus* is the most well-known, can be found in the tropical regions of America. *Urania sloanus* can be recognised immediately because of its very long tails. Furthermore, this butterfly looks very similar to its African counterpart *Chrysiridia*. The bright blue, black and white-coloured caterpillars of the *Urania* butterflies feed on poisonous plants of the genus *Omphalea* (Euphorbiaceae). The distinctive colour pattern of the caterpillar and butterfly warns insect eaters that they are inedible. *Urania sloanus* is, with its wingspan of less than 6.5 centimetres, a small representative of this family.

Zygaenidae - Burnet Moths

Adscita statices, *Forester*

Adscita statices

Adscita statices, Forester (Zygaenidae family), can be found in a large part of Europe. The butterfly likes open spaces in wooded areas where its host plant, sorrel (*Rumex* sp.), grows. The butterfly lays its eggs in groups. The caterpillars live inside the leaf. When the caterpillar is fully grown, it hibernates. In spring, it pupates in a cocoon on the host plant. There is one generation a year. The butterflies fly in the summer. During the day, they are active and search for flowers.

Caterpillar of Zygaena filipendulae

Zygaena filipendulae

Zygaena filipendulae, Six-spot Burnet (Zygaenidae family), can be found throughout Europe and in the western part of Asia. There is one generation a year. The butterflies fly in June, July and August. The caterpillars hibernate. The following spring, when they are fully grown, they pupate in an elongated cocoon on the stalk of a plant. The butterflies and caterpillars of the Six-spot Burnet contain hydrocyanic acid compounds which make them inedible to birds.

Zygaena trifolii

Zygaena trifolii (Zygaenidae family), can be found spread throughout North Africa, Europe and the western part of Asia. The butterflies fly during the day in June and at the beginning of July. The caterpillar's host plants are various species of bird's-foot trefoil (*Lotus* sp.). The caterpillars hibernate. The following spring when

Zygaena trifolii

they are fully grown, they pupate in a cocoon on the stalk of a plant. The butterflies look very much like Six-spot Burnet. Like these butterflies, they also contain poisonous hydrocyanic acid compounds which makes them inedible to birds.

255

Index of Latin names

Index of Terms and Common English Names

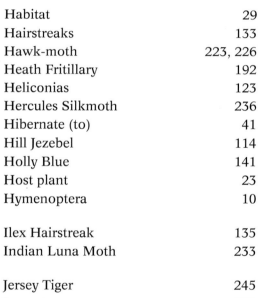

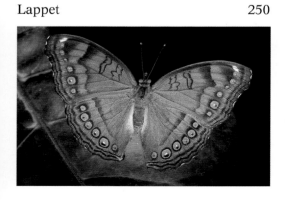

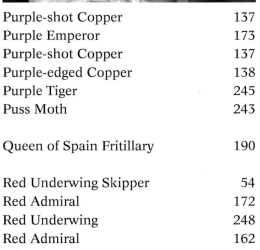

Bibliography

A guide to the butterflies of Zambia, E. Pinhey and I.Loe

A selection of the butterflies of Sri Lanka, J. Banks and J. Banks

Atlas de las mariposas diurnas de Cuba, P. Alayo and L.R. Hernandez

Butterflies of Australia, I.F.B. Common and D.F. Waterhouse

Butterflies of the Bulolo-Wau Valley, M. Parsons

Butterfly culture, J.L.S. Stone and H.J. Midwinter

Ecological atlas van de dagvlinders van Noordwest-Europa, F.A. Bink

Florida butterflies, E.J. Gerberg and R.H. Arnett

Het grote vlinderhandboek, H.L. Lewis

The butterflies of Costa Rica and their natural history, P.J. DeVries

The dictionary of butterflies and moths, A.Watson and P.E.S. Whalley

Threatened swallowtail butterflies and moths, N.M. Collins and M.G. Morris

Vlinders van Europa, David Carter and Roger Philips